LUNA GLOBAL MEDIA

Suncrest Dv. Melbourne, FL

+1 312 212 3899 U.S.

https://lunaglobalmedia.com/

Hijacked Nation, Donald Trump's attack on America's greatness.

ISBN (Paperback): 979-8-9909829-8-7

Printed in the United States of America

Hijacked Nation, Donald Trump's attack on America's greatness.

Bob Gatty
CJ Waldron

Tables of Contents

Foreword

A 4-Letter Word Saves America

It took just four years for the United States of America to lose its luster, and for the brilliant shine of a nation envied around the world to be tarnished by the actions of a president thirsting for power and adulation, and motivated by pure, unadulterated greed.

Over those four years, much of the nation that once had been a beacon of hope for those seeking to achieve a better life and better future for themselves and their children, became obsessed with exclusion, determined to wall themselves off in protectionism.

The nation that had just experienced eight hopeful years of increasing prosperity under its first Black president became riven with discord as racism and White nationalism were given credence and support led by Donald J. Trump, the president of the United States.

Gains that had been made to improve conditions for all Americans, including health care, were attacked even as America was stricken with the coronavirus pandemic resulting in 225,027 deaths as of Nov. 3, 2020, the day of an election largely defined by that pandemic and the failure of the Trump administration to effectively cope with it.

That was the day when the reign of Donald John Trump unraveled as record numbers of Americans, sick of his hateful and incompetent presidency, cast their ballots – many of them by mail. When it was over, when the multitude of unfounded court challenges finally ended and the Electoral

College voted on December 12, there was no serious or credible denial of his defeat. Then, desperate efforts by many Republicans in Congress to overturn the election and restore Trump to the Presidency via the January 6, 2021, MAGA mob attack on the U.S. Capitol summarily failed.

And so, a 4-letter word — VOTE — saved America as Democrat Joe Biden became President of the United States, bringing his message of unity and promise to return America to the land of hope, fairness, and opportunity, rather than Trump's land of hate and division. And just a heartbeat away from the Oval Office was Vice President Kamala Harris, the mixed-race senator from California, whose very selection by Biden shattered America's most venerable political glass ceiling.

In real-time essays by writers Bob Gatty and CJ Waldron, the reader is carried through these historic events as they unfolded, including Biden 's withdrawal from the campaign and Harris' ultimate challenge to Trump, all from the pages of https://notfakenews.biz and its successor https://leanto-theleft.net.

Overview

More Americans voted in 2020 than in any presidential election in the past 120 years despite the ravages of the Covid-19 pandemic that forced America to huddle in their homes for much of 2020 and avoid public contact.

Two-thirds of all eligible voters cast ballots, either by mail, by voting early at new locations created in many communities because of the pandemic, or at the polls on Election Day, Nov. 3. Many stood in line for hours, often in inclement weather and otherwise difficult circumstances to exercise this right so integral to our democracy.

It was a remarkable turnout given those conditions, but even more so because of the tactics of voter suppression used principally by the Republican Party to hold down the turnout in precincts across the nation deemed to be unfriendly to Donald Trump, as well as their down ballot candidates.

A major factor that opened the voter suppression floodgates was the 2013 U.S Supreme Court ruling in *Shelby County v. Holder* that tossed the "preclearance" requirement from the federal Voting Rights Act. No longer do states with a history of racist disenfranchisement need to obtain federal permission to make changes in their voting laws or regulations. Following the *Shelby* decision, many states closed polling places in predominantly Black and Latino communities, with Texas and Georgia, both of which had been subject to federal preclearance, leading the way.

It was a desperation play by the White political establishment in both of those states. In Texas, non-Hispanic White people are now only

40 percent of the population, while Whites represent two-thirds of the state's congressional delegation and the state legislature. Trump won that state's 38 electoral votes with a six-point victory over Biden.

Imposing restrictions designed to make it harder for people who are unlikely to support those in power to vote is nothing new, but since the election of Barack Obama in 2008 there has been a wave of laws make it read intended to do exactly that.

For example, after Obama won Indiana in 2008 with the help of people of color in Indianapolis, the state closed early voting centers there and opened more in predominantly White communities. Since 2020, 24 states have adopted voting restrictions, including the closing of polling places in predominantly Black and Latino communities.

In Georgia, now a battleground state, disenfranchisement tactics prevented a Black woman, Stacey Abrams, from becoming governor. Republican Secretary of State Brian Kemp, who defeated her, was the architect of those tactics.

Nevertheless, Georgia gave former Vice President Joe Biden its 16 electoral votes in a razor thin victory over Trump — by about 12,000 votes out of more than 5 million cast. Abrams is credited with orchestrating Biden's victory by engineering an astounding campaign to encourage Democrats, with a focus on Black voters, to cast their ballots.

Of course, there are other tactics being employed beyond simply closing polling locations. In Florida, Republican officials require people convicted of a felony to pay all court fines and fees before they can vote. In other states, absentee ballots must contain a signature on the outside envelope, and your ballot must be placed in an additional security envelope. If a voting official decides your signature doesn't match, your ballot can be tossed. If you forgot to use the security envelope, your ballot can be tossed.

All those issues played a part in the 2020 election and in Donald Trump's ill-fated court challenges in which he sought to toss out the votes of millions of Americans in states where he lost.

Trump laid the groundwork for those challenges long before the election, warning that voting by mail would be an invitation to fraud and that many ballots would arrive too late to be counted. To make certain that would happen, he installed a lackey as Postmaster General and soon the mails were delayed causing uncertainty about whether mailed-in ballots would be counted. Ultimately, it was clear that early voters and those who voted by mail were predominantly Biden supporters and those who voted at polling places on Election Day were predominantly Trump voters.

While voter suppression tactics may have partially reduced Biden's victory margin, they did not make Trump a winner. There was little dispute that Black voters helped elect Biden by voting in strong numbers, helping him to win in such critical battleground states as Pennsylvania, Georgia, Wisconsin and Michigan. Black voters were simply fed up with Trump's racist rhetoric and actions during his presidency. As we recounted in Volume 1 of *Hijacked Nation*, *Donald Trump's attack on America's greatness,* there seemed to be no end to his racist depravity, even as he bragged that he had done more for Black Americans than any president since Abraham Lincoln.

Black voters comprised 11 percent of the national electorate, and nine in 10 of them supported Biden. While those numbers are like the support generated by Democrat Hillary Clinton in 2016, the difference is that Biden drew more voters in areas with large Black populations. Those included Wayne County, MI, which includes Detroit, Milwaukee County, WI, Philadelphia, PA, and, of course, Atlanta, GA. With victories in those states, Biden was elected with 306 electoral votes against Trump's 232 – exactly the same margin by which Trump defeated Clinton in the 2026 victory that he termed a landslide.

And so, with that remarkable turnout, in an election conducted during a pandemic and despite unending efforts to suppress Biden supporters' votes, Donald Trump was defeated, and that four-letter word, VOTE, saved our nation from four more years of his disastrous presidency.

Chapter One

Election Denial and the Insurrection

Refusing to accept the fact that he was defeated in the 2020 election, Donald Trump rallied his MAGA supporters to Washington where, on January 6, 2021, they attempted to force Vice President Mike Pence to overturn the legitimate election results and restore him to the presidency. That strategy had its beginnings well before the November 3 election.

Trump's Re-election Strategy: Hate and Fear

June 22, 2020

By Bob Gatty

With America now in a full-blown recession, President Trump has shifted his campaign strategy to exploiting latent feelings of hate and fear that he apparently believes can propel him to a second four-year term in the White House.

Skyrocketing unemployment and dramatic stock market losses resulting from coronavirus shutdowns have blasted to smithereens Trump's strategy of claiming to be responsible for the greatest economy in the history of the universe. So now, it's a return to his tried-and-true mantra of turning people against one another -- precisely at a time when America cries out for a healer at the helm, not a divider.

1

His ranting-and-raving speech in Tulsa, OK, Saturday night contained the makings of what can be expected from Trump and his political supporters until the November 3 general election.

Today, 122,000 Americans have lost their lives to covid-19, about 2,000 deaths since Saturday night. What did Trump have to say about that?

First, he said he had told his administration to test fewer people so fewer infections would be found. When he ran into a buzzsaw of criticism for that comment, he later claimed he was just joking, one of his typical fallback excuses. Like the time when he suggested people should ingest disinfectants to ward off the coronavirus, for example. When #cloroxDon hit Twitterdom with a vengeance, he backtracked and said was just being funny.

Apparently feeling sorry for himself, Trump said that when things go wrong, critics "always blame a president." However, he added, "Other than all of the horrible, horrible deaths, people are going to say 'Man, this guy is doing a good job."

But the Biden campaign did not let that one get away. They put out a statement lambasting Trump, saying that "as the American people suffer through rising coronavirus cases and fight to get back to work and get our economy back on track, Donald Trump made one of the most damning admissions in presidential history: that he ordered federal officials to slow down testing just to artificially suppress numbers and conceal his atrocious mismanagement of the worst public health crisis in generations."

"It wasn't a joke: it was a confession," the Biden statement said. "Donald Trump just announced to the entire country that he cares more about saving his job than he does about saving lives or building our economy back. And that is unforgiveable."

But Trump's "testing" joke, stupid as it was, was nothing compared to the rest of his rhetoric meant to stoke fear and division among the races as he called racial justice demonstrators "thugs" and attacked efforts to take down Confederate statues as an assault on "our heritage."

"If you want to save your heritage, you want to save that beautiful heritage of ours, we have a great heritage, we're a great country," he said.

As Slate reported:

Trump encouraged the crowd to boo reporters in the arena, calling them "the most dishonest people anywhere on earth." He denounced athletes who knelt for the national anthem. He claimed that anarchists were really Democrats: "Democrat, all Democrat. Everything I tell you is Democrat." He insulted Rep. Alexandria Ocasio-Cortez ("She doesn't have a clue") and threatened D.C. Mayor Muriel Bowser. "They ripped down a statue … with our radical left mayor watching on television," Trump fumed. "That's going to be very expensive for D.C. They're always looking for money" from the federal government, he said, ominously. "So, it's not going to be good for Mayor Bowser."

Trump directed slurs and insinuations at several ethnic groups. He called the coronavirus "Kung Flu." He railed against undocumented immigrants and vowed to abolish DACA. He pitted black Americans against Latin Americans, claiming that former Vice President Joe Biden had "hollowed out our middle class, including our black middle class, with open borders." He compared murders in Baltimore and Detroit to Guatemala and El Salvador. He speculated that some of the people who had caused trouble in Minneapolis during the George Floyd protests "aren't even from our nation." He described a hypothetical home invader this way: "It's one o'clock in the morning, and a very tough—I've used the word on occasion, hombre—a very tough hombre is breaking into the window of a young woman whose husband is away."

So, this is what we can expect from Trump over the next four months, and perhaps worse. It will not be pretty, but if we all do our job on November 3, it will then be over, and this tyrant will be kicked to the curb where he belongs.

◆ ◆ ◆

Trump's Election Kill Shot?

By Bob Gatty

September 21, 2020

It's becoming increasingly clear that Donald Trump is doing everything possible to rig the presidential election, and the opportunity to pack the Supreme Court with a new conservative justice could be his kill shot.

On Saturday, Trump said during a North Carolina rally that he is "counting on the federal court system" to ensure that the winner is called on election night, November 3, even though millions of ballots will be submitted by mail and may not be counted until days, or even weeks, later.

"We're gonna have a victory on November 3rd the likes of which you've never seen," said Trump. "Now we're counting on the federal court system to make it so we can actually have an evening where we know who wins."

What does that statement tell you?

Trump understands that millions of Biden supporters will be voting by mail and because his supporters are less concerned than Biden's about the coronavirus, they are more likely to vote in-person than Democrats. Election analysts caution that the map that is expected to show solid red on Election Night for a resounding Trump victory, will, however, be a mirage.

"The data is going to show on election night, an incredible victory for Donald Trump. That is likely what to be what we see," said Josh Mendelsohn, who leads the Michael Bloomberg-funded data analytics agency Hawkfish. "When every legitimate vote is counted, and we get to that final day, which will be the Sunday after election day, it will in fact show that what happened on election night was exactly that, a mirage".

And so, Trump's campaign will try to use the federal courts to turn that "red mirage" into reality by making the Election Day vote the official result, ensuring his victory while disenfranchising millions of Americans who vote by mail.

It also indicates that Trump believes he will lose if all votes are counted and Republican efforts to suppress the vote fail.

"This is an open admission that Trump hopes to use the Supreme Court to steal the election," said Rep. Don Beyer (D-VA) on Twitter.

If he succeeds in adding a new conservative ally on the Supreme Court, his position could be strengthened if Election Day challenges reach the high court for a final decision. So, in effect, getting a new Justice appointed could be Trump's kill shot weapon in his plan to steal the election.

Numerous states allow for mail-in votes to be counted after the election.

For example, a Michigan state judge ruled Friday that absentee ballots postmarked before Election Day can be counted up to 14 days later. The Pennsylvania Supreme Court has ruled that ballots postmarked by 8 p.m. on Election Day can be counted up to three days later. And, California has a new law that allows ballots postmarked by Election Day to be counted up to 17 days later.

Trump has claimed for months that voting by mail leads to massive voter fraud, despite the fact that there is no evidence of such a claim, even as he has devised his own plans to rig the election. His new postmaster general imposed new controls on mail delivery that resulted in delays and accusations that the action was being taken to put mailed-in ballots at risk. A federal court in Washington State ruled last week that those steps must be rescinded.

Washington State Chief U.S. District Judge Stanley A. Bastian ruled that Trump and Postmaster General Louis DeJoy were "involved in a politically motivated attack on the efficiency of the Postal Service."

So, the stakes are incredibly high as Democrats seek to delay the Senate confirmation vote for the new Supreme Court justice until after the new president is sworn in.

It could mean the difference between Trump being returned to office with the power of a dictator, or the election of Joe Biden and a return to decent and sensible leadership for our nation.

November 3.

◆ ◆ ◆

The Trump Coup?

By Bob Gatty

Nov 10, 2020

Is Donald Trump, with his several lawsuits claiming election fraud and Attorney General William P. Barr authorizing U.S. attorneys to investigate such claims, engineering a coup that would keep him in power despite his loss to Joe Biden?

That scenario was graphically painted today in an opinion piece by Miami, FL attorney Todd Michaels, published in News & Guts, a news, media, and production company created by journalism icon Dan Rather. Michaels writes as follows:

This is an attempted theft of an election. The Constitution, states' laws, and precedent indicates that if there was indeed a legitimate dispute and a state couldn't certify their election by December 14, state legislatures could use that "uncertainty" to select their own slate of electors.

There are Republican state legislatures in Georgia, Michigan, Wisconsin, Pennsylvania, Arizona. Trump doesn't need to win in Court. He simply needs to tie things up in enough of those states until December 14 when legislatures appoint electors to cast ballots for their states.

That is why he is claiming fraud and irregularities with no evidence. He told us months ago that if he lost the election, he was going to do this. He is now doing it. It's all about his own power, and he would sacrifice our country for it. Sure, if there were legitimate issues he has a right to have those determined. What he doesn't have a right to do is use the Constitution to destroy the Constitution. That's what he is doing.

Michaels' theory is not new. Such a strategy has been discussed online and in the media as a distinct possibility, but for many observers it seemed too far-fetched to be of concern. But consider what Trump also is doing:

He's fired Defense Secretary Mark Esper who had clashed with Trump over his efforts to draw the Defense Department into domestic politics, and CIA Director Gina Haspel and FBI Director Christopher A. Wray could well be next.

He refuses to allow federal officials to cooperate with President-elect Biden's transition team, which stymies their ability to form a new government at a pivotal time in our country's history.

He is supported in his efforts to drag out the election outcome by Republican leaders, such as Senate Majority Leader Mitch McConnell (KY) and Sen. Lindsey Graham (SC) among others. Graham, chairman of the Senate Judiciary Committee, said his committee would investigate "all credible allegations of voting irregularities and misconduct."

Is all of this simply coincidence, or is it a shrewd orchestrated effort by Trump to delay matters until the states appoint their electors, with key GOP-controlled state legislatures appointing Trump supporters who would cast their votes for Trump, defying the actual vote outcome in their states?

Some have suggested that all of this is simply to give Trump "an off ramp", to be able to say that he's not a loser, that the election was stolen from him. A way to soothe his bruised ego. White House sources have been quoted as saying that he will finally give it up, perhaps by this coming weekend, according to MSNBC today.

But until that happens, there is reason to be concerned. Donald Trump actually could be trying to engineer a coup to hold onto power, an act that would destroy our democracy, as guaranteed by the Constitution, for which Trump has shown nothing but disdain.

Wrote Attorney Michaels:

Even if democracy wins, this puts the Country and its continuity in peril. This is the time to fight like our future is at stake. It is. It's incumbent on all people—including Trump supporters and Republican electeds to put the Country and the Constitution before his power, to not allow him to create a crisis in order to maintain power in the face of an electoral defeat. Or America is no more. That's not hyperbole. The Founders would be horrified.

◆◆◆

American Carnage

By C J Waldron

Jan 11, 2021

The term "American Carnage" was introduced into our lexicon during Trump's inauguration speech four years ago. It was a reference to the lower-class neighborhoods and minorities he and his base viewed as "infesting" America. It was a call to Make America White Again and it culminated in the deadly insurrection that Trump instigated Jan. 6, 2021, in a vain attempt to remain in power.

Like December 7th and September 11th, January 6th will go down as another date of infamy. It will forever be known as Insurrection Day; the day a sitting president and his supporters sought to violently overthrow the government.

Relying on a campaign of lies, misinformation and flawed conspiracy theories spread by right wing media, the plan was to force Congress to overturn the election of President Biden and install Donald Trump as leader, presumably with dictatorial powers.

Make no mistake, this attempted coup was nothing less than an uprising to elevate white supremacists and re-take their version of America from "the brown people" and those from "shithole countries" who "stole" the election. The Proud Boys, Oath Keepers, Q-anon and other lesser white supremacist groups stormed the Capitol with the intent of taking Vice President Mike Pence and members of Congress hostage, or worse, and forcing them to negate the election results.

The seeds of this coup attempt were planted long ago.

From Trump's "very fine people" when referencing the white supremacists in Charlottesville, to his condemnation of Black Lives Matter and the false narrative that those athletes protesting by kneeling during the National Anthem or taking to the streets to protest the murders of George Floyd, Breonna Taylor and many others, Trump was egging on his followers to refuse to accept the likelihood that he would lose the 2020 presidential election.

The Insurrection of January 6th will go down as one of the biggest international failures since 9/11. For weeks the internet was buzzing with chatter about an event in Washington that would coincide with the certification of Biden's victory. Trump even spurred on the budding calamity by scheduling a rally and inviting his base to DC for a "wild" event via Twitter.

Calls for violence and armed insurrection were ignored, leading many to question whether the lack of police presence meant the revolt was an inside job. The relative ease by which the rioters were able to gain access to the Capitol, the gentle treatment when they were pushed back and the lack of a greater police presence contrasts greatly with how the Black Lives Matter protestors were treated when tear gas and rubber bullets were used on peaceful protestors so Trump could have a photo op.

On a related note, the Secret Service is changing the presidential protection detail out of fear that some of the current agents might be Trump loyalists and undermine the Biden administration.

In the aftermath of the attack, Republicans continued their hopeless quest to overturn the election results. Senators Ted Cruz (R-TX) and Josh Hawley (R-MO), joined by over one hundred Republican members of the House of Representatives, refused to admit defeat and instead dragged the process of certifying Biden's victory into the wee hours of the morning. Their pointless efforts only highlighted the hypocrisy of Republicans who, following the attack, were asking for unity as Democrats proceeded with Articles of Impeachment.

Actions have consequences. Major corporations, the lifeblood of campaign finance, have halted donations to Republicans who voted to overturn the election results. Perhaps that was the reason for the about face many Republicans made?

What's next? As mentioned above, Democrats, and possibly with some Republican support, are proceeding with impeachment proceedings if Vice President Pence refuses to invoke the 25th Amendment or Trump fails to resign.

Meanwhile, more arrests are being made following the insurrection. They actually weren't that hard to find because they posted their illegal actions on social media or were spotted, sans masks, trespassing in the halls of the Capitol.

Further investigation showed that the attack could have been far more violent. Police found pipe bombs, Molotov cocktails and weapons that fortunately never made it inside the building. Rioters were spotted with zip ties, with the presumed aim of taking members of Congress hostage, or worse. (Some theorized that the foiled abduction of Michigan Governor Gretchen Whitmer was a "dry run" for what was being planned in Congress).

Despite overwhelming evidence many, including Trump sycophant Matt Gaetz (R-FL), pushed the baseless claims that it was actually Antifa that was behind the insurrection. It seems some people just can't stop lying no matter what happens.

With Inauguration Day drawing closer, Trump is facing increasing demands to resign or otherwise be removed prior to the end of his term. There is also increasing chatter that the insurrectionists will return to Washington on Inauguration Day to disrupt the proceedings. Trump had his Twitter account permanently suspended because Twitter viewed his tweet about not attending the inauguration as a signal to his supporters that it was safe to wreak havoc on the ceremonies.

As Trump's time in office comes to a close, he faces numerous legal battles and financial woes that predate his time in office. He now faces the additional potential of being charged with his role in inciting the insurrection.

Even as he denied his election defeat and took unprecedented steps to prevent the peaceful transition of power, Trump had visions of his post-presidential life. He saw himself as making a tremendous comeback in 2024 as he installed loyalists to hinder the Biden administration. He saw himself as king-maker, holding tremendous sway over the Republican Party as he conducted his own shadow presidency. He saw a Trump dynasty as his loyal supporters would elect his children to offices for which they had zero qualifications.

All of this evaporated with the events of the past week. Many Republicans are shying away from him and his loyal base is also dwindling as many face incarceration for their involvement in the insurrection.

If life where to imitate art, Trump should be forced to endure his own Walk of Shame a la *Game of Thrones.*

Perhaps Trump's mention of American Carnage was prescient. We are indeed facing unprecedented carnage as the coronavirus pandemic ravages the nation. Thousands are dying daily due to his administration's inept response and abysmal vaccine roll-out.

And now he can add six more deaths to his ledger of shame as five people, including a Capitol police officer died during the riots and a sixth committed suicide following the horrific events.

The country will eventually heal, as we always have. But it will be a hard lesson. We will need to confront our inner demons and the ugliness that lies in the hearts of many Americans. Only then will there be an end to the American Carnage.

◆◆◆

One Nation Under Siege

By C J Waldron

Jan 14, 2021

As it turns out, the January 6 attack on the Capitol was only the first salvo of the Trump Insurrection. Even as the rioters were leaving Washington, they were already planning to return on or about January 20th to disrupt the inauguration ceremony of President-elect Joe Biden.

The white supremacist group, the Boogaloos have planned a January 17 protest and several groups are reported to be scheming to hold armed protests in all 50 state capitals from January 17 through the 20th.

Lawmakers are continuing their efforts to have Trump removed from office prior to the end of his term. They are also striving to strip Trump of the perks afforded to ex-presidents, which include a lifetime salary as well as a lifetime stipend for travel. If convicted by the Senate, Trump would also be banned from running for office again, as he was planning to do in 2024.

Meanwhile, Republicans, who fueled the insurrection with their refusal to acknowledge the election results and baseless claims of voter fraud, are now calling for unity in the wake of Trump's second impeachment. As threats of more acts of violence and insurrection continue , Republicans, and the Insurrectionist-in-Chief, are claiming that Democrats are stoking "tremendous anger" while alternately saying they condemn violence. They are making false claims that the insurrectionists were actually Antifa and comparing the events of January 6 to the Black Lives Matter protests in Portland or Seattle.

And yet they have the hypocrisy to call for unity after they've voted to deny the election results of those states where Trump lost.

It's not unity they want. Instead, they want to ignore the facts. They want to ignore that Trump incited insurrection and the violent overthrow of the government. Like the past impeachment, they are taking to the airwaves to claim, once again, that impeachment isn't necessary because Trump has learned his lesson.

And while the nation is under siege, Trump is facing numerous personal battles of his own.

In addition to the legal issues he already faces in the Southern District of New York, which are aimed at uncovering Trump's financial crimes, he is facing further financial woes as almost a billion dollars in debt comes due when he leaves office. The recent insurrection has caused his primary lender, Deutsche Bank to sever ties, cutting off a major influx of cash. Major corporations are also cutting off funding to Trump, along with members of Congress who opposed certification of Biden's victory.

Still, we remain a nation under siege.

With Trump being impeached for a second time, there are still those who did not vote to impeach, not because they believed him, but that they and their families were receiving death threats. In the coming days and weeks, we will see if, once he is out of office, these hate groups will once again fade into the background. Or not.

Until then, we remain one nation...under siege.

❖ ❖ ❖

Was the U.S. Capitol Attack an Inside Job?

By Bob Gatty

Jan 15, 2021

Could it possibly be that some Republican members of Congress are so demented that they conspired with the domestic terrorists who attacked the Capitol Jan. 6, threatening the lives of their colleagues and Vice President Mike Pence?

There is increasing anecdotal evidence that this could be the case and that those who planned and carried out the attack were also supported by some members of law enforcement who helped to facilitate their madness.

It was announced today that internal investigators for the departments of Justice, Defense, Interior, and Homeland Security will investigate how security officials prepared for and responded to the pro-Trump rally that preceded the deadly riot. Questions to be answered include how the Capitol, with so many security agencies available, could be overcome by a mob with bats, bear repellent, plastic handcuffs, and simply brute force.

But beyond questions of poor planning and failure to heed clear advance warnings that a violent uprising would take place, there have been reports that some lawmakers may have somehow abetted the mob attack. Some reportedly provided tours of the Capitol the day before the attack to individuals who used those visits as reconnaissance to determine who was where and how to get there.

Meanwhile, Democrats have called for allegations that GOP members of Congress encouraged the attempted insurrection.

"Their accomplices in this House will be held responsible," Rep. Jerrold Nadler (D-N.Y.) said in a speech during the impeachment debate.

Rep. Mikie Sherrill (D-N.J.) said in a Facebook Live broadcast that she saw Republicans "who had groups coming through the Capitol that I saw on Jan. 5 for reconnaissance for the next day." She said some of her GOP colleagues "abetted" Trump and "incited this violent crowd." "I'm going to see that they're held accountable and, if necessary, ensure that they don't serve in Congress," she said.

Rep. Lauren Boebert (R-CO), who carries a Glock and supports the QAnon movement, was reported to be one of those providing reconnaissance tours for individuals who participated in the riots. She is facing a backlash for live-tweeting House Speaker Nancy Pelosi's (D-CA) location during the attack.

Shortly after Trump's supporters stormed the Capitol, Boebert tweeted: "We were locked in the House Chambers. The Speaker has been removed from the chambers."

Said one Twitter user:

"@FBIWFO please arrest @laurenboabert for aiding and abetting those who were hunting down @SpeakerPelosi on Jan 6th by tweeting the Speaker's whereabouts. "She's 5ft tall, 100 pounds and carries a Glock (and won't stop telling everyone)."

Another Twitter user cited the 14th Amendment to the Constitution, stating:

"No person shall be a Senator or Representative in Congress, who, having previously taken an oath, as a member of Congress to support the Constitution of the United States, shall have engaged in insurrection or rebellion against the same."

"You can't get more explicit than that," tweeted a third. "Expulsion of Boebert is only the start. Indictment has to follow quickly."

One Democratic Congresswoman, Rep. Ayanna Pressley (MA), said the panic buttons installed in her office suite in case of emergencies had been ripped out. That report is now being investigated, according to her office.

"Every panic button in my office had been torn out -- the whole unit," Chief of Staff Sarah Groh told the *Boston Globe*.

Obviously, assuming that was related to the insurrectionists' attack, it had to be premeditated and likely either performed by, or facilitated by, individuals with access to the lawmaker's locked office.

And, while all of this was happening, Sen. Josh Hawley (R-MO), who started the Republican opposition to seating Biden's electors, was photographed giving a clenched fist salute to the rioters.

Hawley was the first senator to support efforts by GOP House members to challenge Biden electors, an act that made the entire charade on Jan. 6 possible, as without support from at least one senator, House members' objections would have fallen flat.

But his self-serving actions have backfired, showing that he badly miscalculated the political wisdom of going to the mat for Trump at the expense of the republic. Trump can now be called the biggest loser, with Hawley close behind.

Presumed to be running for President in 2024, Hawley has lost major donors and supporters and a book deal; his home state newspaper said he had "blood on his hands"; thousands of law school alumni and students have pushed for him to be disbarred; and at least one Democratic senator has called for his resignation, reported *The Washington Post*.

The fact that he broke the dam, so to speak, in the Senate led to other opportunists like Sen. Ted Cruz (TX) jumping on the bandwagon, and then, eventually, to several more GOP senators who pushed the false Trump narrative of election fraud, giving credence to his claims and spurring on the right-wing crazies who took up the defeated president's call to "fight." So, was it an inside job, that day when at least five people, including two police officers and a QAnon supporter died in the violent mob attack? When legislators led those would-be terrorists on their Capitol tours on Jan. 5, were they just being nice to encourage the support of constituents? Or did they know what they were doing and were they part of the planning that led to death and destruction that fateful day?

When Hawley and Cruz and the others who insisted on objecting to the Biden electors in key states did that, they had to know their actions would have consequences. And then, even after the riot, Hawley doubled down, unapologetic about questioning the election results. He did that despite Senate Majority Leader Mitch McConnell's (R-KY) warning that the end result of their gambit, if successful, would be to send democracy into "a death spiral."

We may never know how close we were to McConnell's prescient warning coming to pass. There were terrorists within the group who intended to harm targeted lawmakers, and even lynch Vice President Pence because, as Trump said, he had failed to show courage and overturn the election as he had demanded.

Trump will soon be gone, but the consequences of this tragedy will remain. And to think that representatives and senators elected by the people, who serve with some of those targeted, may have been complicit in this traitorous and deadly tragedy is almost too much to contemplate.

◆◆◆

The Geniuses of the Insurrection

By Bob Gatty

Mar 3, 2021

On January 6, defeated President Donald Trump encouraged thousands of his supporters gathered at the White House to go to the U.S. Capitol and convince lawmakers to overturn Joe Biden's election. They went, but arrest records show that Trump did not exactly send his best and brightest to do his dirty work on that January day.

Some 300 have since been arrested because of the attempted insurrection that resulted in five deaths and then, later, the suicide of two Capitol Hill police officers. They were people who believed Trump's false claims that the election was stolen from him and that it was their duty to fight, as he encouraged them to do.

They were duped by Trump and now some apparently are planning a return visit sometime between tomorrow and Saturday, when they believe Trump will magically return to power. So Capitol Hill is still an armed camp, with thousands of National Guard troops deployed there and a razor wire topped fence surrounding the Capitol grounds. And the U.S. House of Representatives is shutting down for the day because of the threat.

It doesn't take a genius to figure out that the supporters of QAnon and various militia groups are idiots for believing such a fantasy. Nevertheless, the threat has been deemed real by the Capitol Police and the FBI and so precautions are being taken.

All of this is part of the increased threat of domestic terrorism which is now "metastasizing" across the nation, according to Senate testimony by FBI Director Christopher A. Wray, who told senators yesterday that the number of investigations and arrests continues to increase.

In his testimony, Wray said the January 6 attack has been "an inspiration to a number of terrorist extremists," both foreign and domestic, adding that Republican claims that antifa was involved in the attack were false.

The 'Trump-Made-Me-Do-It' Defense

Now, many of those who were arrested on charges stemming from the attack are trying to use as a defense that they were simply doing what Trump told them to do -- the "Trump-made-me-do-it" defense, as reported by the Associated Press. However, that's not going to fly, if one judge's decision is any indication.

18

Said U.S. District Judge Beryl Howell, "This purported defense, if recognized, would undermine the rule of law because then, just like a king or a dictator, the president could dictate what's illegal and what isn't in this country. And that is not how we operate here."

Judge Howell then ordered pretrial detention of William Chrestman, a suspected member of the Kansas City-area chapter of the Proud Boys. Chrestman's attorneys claimed Trump gave the mob "explicit permission and encouragement" to attack, thus providing those who obeyed him with "a viable defense against criminal liability."

"It is an astounding thing to imagine storming the United States Capitol with sticks and flags and bear spray, arrayed against armed and highly trained law enforcement. Only someone who thought they had an official endorsement would even attempt such a thing. And a Proud Boy who had been paying attention would very much believe he did," Chrestman's lawyers wrote.

The 13 Idiots

Clearly, many of those involved in the insurrection had failed their high school civics courses because they somehow believed that the election results could be overturned by Vice President Pence, as Trump had requested, or by Congress. In fact, *The Washington Post* today cited the cases of the "13 not so greatest hits from the Capitol riot arrest records" in an article by @ AaronBlake. Here's his summary:

13. Kevin Loftus: Allegedly posted a selfie in the Capitol with the caption, "One of 700 inside," adding, "That's right folks some of us are in it to win it." He later posted to Facebook, upon seeing himself pictured among the suspects, "I am wanted by the FBI for illegal entry", pointing to his photo.

12. Troy Faulkner: Allegedly wore a jacket from his painting company that included a phone number. Hello!

11. Derrick Evans: The now-former West Virginia state lawmaker allegedly live-streamed himself entering the Capitol and identified himself: "We're in! Derrick Evans is in the Capitol!"

10. Joshua Lollar: Allegedly posted to Facebook after the Capitol riot saying, "Yeah, I'm good. Just got gassed and fought with cops that I never thought would happen." Someone believed to be his sister posted, "We cleaned off the post of you going into and inside the capital since they plan to prosecute everyone that was in there." A minute later, she added, "You need to clean off your page."

9. Guy Reffitt: Allegedly told his family that he had been in the Capitol and had brought his gun with him. His adult son told investigators that his father later began to try covering his tracks, including deleting footage from his GoPro, and issued threats to his family if they turned him in. Among the charges in his indictment is witness tampering.

8. William Robert Norwood III: Allegedly dressed like antifa to avoid arrest and told friends and family he had gotten away with it before being arrested. "I'll look just like ANTIFA," he said. "I'll get away with anything." Later, he wrote, "It worked. I got away with things that others were shot or arrested for."

7. Kevin Lyons: Allegedly briefly posted an Instagram of himself in House Speaker Nancy Pelosi's (D-CA) office saying, "WHOSE HOUSE?!?!? OUR HOUSE!!" He later told the FBI he had a dream about being in the Capitol that day, before they showed him the Instagram. "Wow, you're pretty good. That was only up for an hour," he said, according to court documents. He later emailed video of his time there, saying, "Hello Nice FBI Lady, Here are the links to the videos."

6. Tam Dinh Pham: Allegedly left photos of himself in the Capitol in the deleted photos section of his phone.

5. Jenna Ryan: Allegedly posted multiple videos from inside the Capitol promoting her real estate business, including saying, "You guys, can you believe this? I'm not messing around. When I come to sell your house, this is what I'll do. I'll ... sell your house."

4. Justin Stoll: Allegedly responded to someone who criticized his videos from inside the Capitol a day afterward by issuing threats, including, "If you ever in your ... existence did something to jeopardize taking me away from my family, you will absolutely meet your maker. ... You can play that for the [prosecutor] in court, I don't care." He's now charged with making threats and witness tampering.

3. Richard Michetti allegedly texted with his ex-girlfriend about being in the Capitol. At one point, he told her she was a "moron" if she didn't understand the election was stolen. She later turned him in.

2. Joshua Matthew Black: Allegedly admitted in a video posted on YouTube — two days after the siege, when others were covering their tracks — that he entered the Capitol with a knife: "We just wanted to get inside the building, I wanted to get inside the building so I could plead the blood of Jesus over it. That was my goal."

1. Thomas Fee: Allegedly sent a selfie from the Capitol to his girl-friend's brother, who had asked if he was in Washington after seeing a social media post. The brother was a federal agent.

Enough said.

◆ ◆ ◆

Who REALLY Won the Insurrection?

By C J Waldron

Jan. 16, 2023

On January 6th, 2021, a mob attacked the U.S. Capitol building in an attempt to halt the certification of Joe Biden as the winner of the 2020 presidential election. Incited by Donald Trump, with his baseless claims of a "rigged system" and a stolen election, they aimed to allow Trump to remain in office, no matter what the voters decided.

It didn't work. Hundreds were arrested and convicted, many on relatively minor charges, for their part in attempts to overthrow the government. While some expressed remorse for their actions, others stuck to their claims and declared themselves political prisoners. They were even backed by some of the very members of Congress they attacked.

Fast forward two years later: Republicans now have a narrow majority in the House. Investigations are moving at a snail's pace, giving the new Republican majority an opportunity to further stall holding the ultimate perpetrators accountable and there are even cries to undo the dual impeachments of Donald Trump in yet another transparent attempt to rewrite the history of that infamous event.

This begs the question, who really won on January 6th?

The Squeaky Wheel

The old saying goes, "The squeaky wheel gets the grease". It's a matter of simple mechanics that, in order for something to work, all its parts must be properly lubricated in order to operate efficiently. And what's true in mechanics is often true in life.

But should it be?

The recent fiasco of selecting the Speaker of the House witnessed a lot of greasing of palms as a small, but influential, group of representatives forced concession after concession in order to gain, not a vote of support, but at least a vote not to oppose Kevin McCarthy's nomination. They are already organizing committees to investigate those who executed the search warrant for illegal documents at Trump's Mar-a-Lago residence. The committee investigating the January 6th insurrection is being disbanded and efforts are being made to erase both impeachments of Donald Trump, while simultaneously launching a vendetta campaign against President Biden.

In education there are often programs aimed at reining in misbehaving students. They are given catchy names like "Catch 'em Being Good". They reward these recalcitrant learners for engaging in behaviors that are normal expectations such as bringing required materials to class or remaining in class three out of five days. They are given special lunches, awarded certain privileges and given deference over those students who are generally well behaved.

Experienced educators look on these programs with a jaundiced eye. Instead of improving student behavior, the once well-behaved students see opportunity in acting out. They see that they can gain more by doing less.

As a result, such programs are doomed to failure. But that doesn't stop well meaning, though misguided, social workers who will repackage these programs in a vain attempt to influence a future crop of students.

Apparently, certain Republican lawmakers were poor students (Take Lauren Boebert as an example) because they are doing exactly what they've come to expect from those in charge. Act up enough and your needs will be met. Sadly, it means they will likely be joined by others who see the benefits of getting their way by bucking the most sensible trend.

This is a perfect example of the squeaky wheel concept, and it's one that the MAGA wing of the Republican Party is adopting to gain advantages in the new House of Representatives. It's also why nothing can be accomplished without catering to this small, but influential, wing of the GOP.

They are Republican's squeaky wheel.

Re-Writing History

Even before the detritus caused by the insurrectionists was cleared, there were those in the very halls where the attacks took place attempting to rewrite history. Despite the violent attacks, they still stuck to their unsubstantiated claims of voting irregularities that conveniently only occurred in the states where Trump lost. There were even efforts put forth to present a slate of alternative electors who would rule in Trump's favor.

Despite myriad banners, flags and red MAGA hats in support of Donald Trump, Republicans tried to place the blame for the insurrection on Antifa, the FBI and members of the Black Lives Matter movement. They disputed whether it was even an insurrection at all (It was), whether it could be called an armed insurrection since no one was carrying firearms (they were), tried to claim those attacking the Capital were no more harmful than a group of tourists, and even called into question Joe Biden's legitimacy as president by continuing to cite vague voter irregularities such as votes being mysteriously changed either by corrupt voting machines or agents from China or Venezuela.

Meanwhile, in sunny Mar-a-Lago, Donald Trump recently launched yet another bid for the White House. He is aiming to become the second person to claim non-consecutive terms in office despite the fact he is still disputing the results of the 2020 election and demanding to be immediately reinstated. He is joined in the Sunshine State by fellow insurrectionist, Brazil's Jair Bolsanaro and his potential 2024 rival, Ron DeSantis.

Historians may argue that, since Trump has refused to concede defeat, he is ineligible to run again in 2024 because the Constitution only permits presidents to hold office for two four-year terms. To run again, it can be argued that Trump must first admit that he lost in 2020. The likelihood of that happening is about as remote as peace in Ukraine.

The back door deals Kevin McCarthy made to gain the position of Speaker of the House are a mystery, but one of the rumors is a promise to "look into" expunging the dual impeachments of Donald Trump. That would definitely be an historic rewrite of history.

The Classified Paper Trail

The recent revelations of classified documents associated with Joe Biden's time as vice president being discovered at multiple locations has Republicans salivating. They want to equate Biden's turning over of multiple classified documents with Trump's refusal to voluntarily surrender such after he left office. They are promising to conduct numerous investigations into the Biden documents while ignoring Trump. They claim there are already several ongoing investigations into the Mar-a-Lago scandal, so they want to deflect attention by focusing on President Biden. While most of the Republicans support this, it is primarily being pushed by the MAGA wing of the party.

The irony is that the twin scandals, which may or may not result in a criminal investigation into both, could prevent either Trump or Biden from running again in 2024, which is exactly what most Americans are seeking.

Who is In Charge?

The looming Federal deficit ceiling could be the first real glimpse of who controls the reins of power in the Republican Party. A group of lawmakers, dubbed the Taliban 20, is threatening to hold the government hostage unless specific demands are met. This is the same group of representatives who repeatedly stymied Kevin McCarthy's ascension to the Speaker's chair until certain issues were addressed. They warn that the same could happen if demands, such as repealing an over of the IRS, aren't included in any pending legislation.

While McCarthy did eventually get the votes he needed, it was at the expense of making certain promises to this recalcitrant minority in the House. So, in essence, it is they, and not Kevin McCarthy, who hold the actual authority in the House. Without them, no significant progress can occur.

This group includes election deniers Jim Jordan, Marjorie Taylor

Green, Lauren Boebert and Matt Gaetz. To gain their votes, or at least not vote against him, McCarthy had to promise them seats on highly influential committees. So, those who supported the Big Lie are the actual power holders in the House.

It's as if they were the true winners of the January 6th insurrection.

◆◆◆

Chapter Two

The 2024 Election

As Americans go to the polls Nov. 5, 2024, their choice is between Donald Trump, a convicted felon who tried to overturn the 2020 election and Vice President Kamala Harris, who was tabbed by President Biden to succeed him after withdrawing from the campaign due to questions about his age, 81 and a disastrous debate with Trump. Harris, a former prosecutor, upended the race and generated considerable excitement, especially among women, people of color, and younger voters. The stage was set when Biden selected Harris as his running mate.

Vice President Kamala Harris

By Bob Gatty

Aug 11, 2020

Sen. Kamala Harris (D-CA), named by former VP Joe Biden to be his vice-presidential running mate, brings with her a sense of compassion, of what's right and wrong, and a determination to set things right after the disastrous Trump administration.

Words that she uttered last summer when she visited Big Mike's Soul Food Restaurant in Myrtle Beach, SC, are as true today, in the midst of the coronavirus pandemic and racial divisions that have been worsened by Donald Trump, as they were then:

"It's about having a vision where we can be unburdened by where we have been," she said. "Let's understand what's happening right now and know that when we show up, it can change." "We love our country and are prepared to fight for it," declared Harris. "This is not only about defeating this guy who is in the White House but fighting for a vision of America where everyone can see themselves."

A vision where everyone can see themselves.

That is exactly what this country needs today, having been ripped apart by Trump's hateful rhetoric and his determination to set people against each other.

The naming of Harris by Biden says a lot about the former vice president. While many considered her to be the obvious choice after he announced that his running mate would be a woman, he took his time and carefully considered many other highly qualified candidates for perhaps the most important decision of his candidacy.

Moreover, he chose a former prosecutor who nearly prosecuted Biden during the Democratic debates when she excoriated him for his long-ago held position on busing. Some pundits thought that might disqualify her from being named.

But no, Biden demonstrated that, unlike Trump, he does not hold grudges and that he makes decisions based on what's best for the country – not based on who may have been mean to him.

While Harris' selection is important politically, as it certainly will help solidify support from women and African Americans, it is even more important for what the future could bring. At 55, she will be serving with Biden, who would be 78 years old by Inauguration Day, and has described himself as a transition candidate.

So, it is entirely possible that she one day could be the President of the United States, the first African American woman, in fact, the first woman to do so.

Vice President Joe Biden has already made history with her selection. It is only the beginning of what is about to unfold.

◆◆◆

A 2024 Nightmare Scenario

By C J Waldron

Nov 7, 2021

Let's fast forward to 2024. The pandemic is over, the economy is once again on solid ground and America has tenuously reclaimed its place on the world stage as the leader of democracy. Unfortunately, things aren't all rosy. The 2022 midterms saw Republicans retake both the House and Senate, and any future strides to improve America, such as the Build Back Better law and the Infrastructure law have been slowed by uncooperative members of the opposition party.

This is nothing new. Republicans did the same to President Obama, and yet were unable to accomplish anything of merit during the four horrific years of the Trump administration. There was no border wall (that Mexico would pay for). There was no simultaneous repeal and replacement of Obamacare. Virtually nothing of consequence happened during those four years other than to further divide America and make us the laughingstock of the world through a series of foreign policy blunders.

Prologue

Republicans did get one thing they wanted with their 2022 midterm victories. They were finally able to move on from the 2020 election. That's not to say there was any level of accountability. Instead, Trump and those

29

involved in the January 6th insurrection were let off with impunity because Republicans immediately shut down any efforts to hold them accountable once they assumed office. The committees, the investigations and the prosecutions were halted, either by disbanding them, or cutting off necessary funding that would allow them to proceed. So, Trump was rewarded for his efforts of lawsuits and delays as he ran out the clock until a more friendly Congress was in place.

So, it's 2024.

Donald Trump has amassed a huge war chest by duping his base into believing the Big Lie of a stolen election. Due to his big crowds, Trump believes he is more popular than ever despite ratings showing the opposite. As he faces yet another showdown with Joe Biden, he believes he will be victorious this time, while he refuses to acknowledge his loss in 2020. Nikki Haley has temporarily abandoned her presidential ambitions and continues on her quixotic quest to have Biden to take a cognitive test to prove that, at 82, he would still be capable of carrying out the tasks necessary to be president. While she claims ALL older politicians should be subject to this requirement, she stops short at requiring it for Trump.

While Trump faces a tremendous challenge from Biden, he is also facing dissension in his own ranks. A faction of the Republican Party, declaring themselves the "Real Republicans", while Trump paradoxically calls them RINOS (Republicans in Name Only), has declared their opposition to Trump's re-election bid. Perhaps it's Adam Kinzinger (R-OH) or Liz Cheney (R-Wy), or some combination of a "dream ticket". Meanwhile, Trump enjoys the support of right-wing whackos like Majorie Taylor Greene (R-GA) and Matt Gaetz (R-FL). Yet, this challenge threatens to siphon Trump's support by giving Republicans an alternative.

Nightmare

This sets up the stage for the nightmare scenario.

While the splinter faction of the Republican Party is unable to garner a victory, it prevents Trump's return to Washington. Predictably, Trump again claims voter fraud and demands that he be awarded the electors who voted for the Republican faction. Yet, it still isn't enough as Joe Biden cruises to a re-election win, creating the typical outcry from Trump supporters. Rather than acknowledge that Trump once again lost, they declare him the "rightful president". They try, and are denied, permission to stage another march on Washington to protest the election results.

Failing to get permission to hold a rally in Washington, Trump supporters organize an "alternative inauguration" in Trump-friendly Florida. They demand Trump be given the "nuclear football" that gives him access to the launch codes necessary to start a nuclear attack. Trump is even recognized as the "rightful victor" by North Korea, Brazil and Venezuela. They insist in recounts and invalidating election results.

This mock inauguration allows Trump to establish his own shadow presidency. This is nothing new since he has yet to concede to the 2020 election as he continues to push the Big Lie. This ongoing fracture garners support from Republican governors and members of Congress, pushing America closer to the brink of another Civil War.

Epilogue

A Democratic victory in the 2022 midterm elections is absolutely essential to preventing this nightmare scenario. Republican controlled legislatures in statehouses are passing laws to make voter suppression legal again. Republicans in Congress are denying true voting reforms by refusing to pass the John Lewis Voting Rights Act. Machinations by Republican run states will give them authority to overturn election results. The appointment of Louis De Joy as Postmaster General threatens to slow down the mail-in voting process, effectively disenfranchising millions of voters.

To preserve democracy, Americans must make their voices heard. The first step is to support Democrats in the midterms. Then, there must be accountability for the January 6th insurrection and a ban on Trump ever holding public office again. By doing this, we can prevent this nightmare from becoming a reality.

◆◆◆

Republicans Need a Red Wave

By C J Waldron

Feb. 8, 2023

The predicted Red Wave that Republicans anticipated during the 2022 midterms never materialized. While they gained just enough to wrest control of the House, they failed to upend the Democratic majority in the Senate.

This means the next two years will be filled with inaction, distractions and pointless investigations and hearings aimed at gaining some measure of revenge for the multiple inquiries, dual impeachments and ongoing criminal proceedings being waged against the Trump administration.

The thing is, Republicans would have truly benefited from a Red Wave; just not the one they wished for.

Had Republicans elected more moderate members instead of those who support the lunatic fringe MAGA agenda, they may have stood a better chance of making an actual difference. Instead, they will continue to be mired in controversy as they are forced to acquiesce to the demands of the far right as they attempt to retake the White House in 2024.

The Republican Party has deviated from its original mission so far that it would be unrecognizable to those who founded it. Despite laying claim to The Party of Lincoln, Honest Abe himself, should he return from the grave, wouldn't know the current incarnation.

History is Written by the Victors

The events of January 6th were viewed on live television for all to see. This hasn't prevented Republicans from trying to re-write history. Despite the mob bearing banners in support of Donald Trump, despite their chants to "Hang Mike Pence" for refusing to go along with the fraudulent efforts to overturn the election, and despite the numerous convictions and guilty pleas, they are still trying to reframe the insurrection by blaming Antifa, comparing it to a normal tourist visit, accusing the FBI of instigating the riots, claiming it wasn't an "armed insurrection" since no one had weapons (they did), and rebranding those who took part as "Patriots".

The Select Committee Investigating the January 6th Insurrection came to the conclusion that Donald Trump was solely to blame for the violence inflicted on the Capitol that day. This conclusion was roundly criticized by Republicans, and even some Democrats, who wanted to address the failures of Capitol security in preventing the riots.

With several of its members no longer in office, the committee was forced to rush its results before it was disbanded by the now Republican-controlled House. Rather than re-initiate these proceedings to address these issues, Republicans instead formed a committee of their own to investigate how Conservatives have been targeted by law enforcement.

The New Face of the Republican Party

In a truly inappropriate sight, QAnon kook Marjorie Taylor Greene was allowed to preside over a session of the House. This was made possible by a devil's bargain that Rep. Kevin McCarthy (R-CA) was forced into to gain the much-coveted speakership he desired. Despite spreading conspiracy theories, threatening Democratic members of the House and harassing survivors of mass casualty attacks, she was rewarded because she stood by McCarthy throughout the marathon voting process.

As if these actions weren't enough, Greene became the de facto leader of the Republican Party when she repeatedly heckled President Biden during his State of the Union speech Feb. 7. Wearing an outfit some compared to Cruella deVille, Greene shouted "Liar!" over and over as Biden pointed out, correctly, that some Republicans have suggested cuts to Social Security.

Ignoring facts, as usual, Greene and several other Republicans booed and heckled as Biden refused to name who (Sen. Rick Scott, R-FL) would make such an outrageous proposal. She later complained that images of her shouting amounted to her being spied on by Democrats who opposed her.

Prior to President Biden's speech, supposed leader McCarthy admonished those in his party, telling them they needed to be respectful during the address. His complete lack of control over his party members was made all the more obvious as he was seen glaring at hecklers and later shushing them like a substitute teacher with little classroom management skills.

Greene demonstrated her appalling lack of Congressional decorum with a lame excuse. She declared, "People stand up and clap for the president. I think we can stand up and oppose what he's saying. Just like a sports team, right?"

Obviously, she can't tell the difference between the halls of government and a high school football game, which begs the question, what is she doing in Congress in the first place?

Republicans were equally tone deaf when they selected former Trump press secretary, and current Arkansas Governor (Is there such a thing as a nepo-politician?), Sarah Huckabee Sanders to give the Republican response to Biden's address. In her typical monotone, she railed against the newest right-wing boogeymen, Critical Race Theory and the deliberately vague Woke agenda. She also took a swipe at Biden's age, apparently unaware (or was she?) that she was also denigrating her former boss and current party front runner in the 2024 election. In a shameless case of self-promotion, she stated that it was time for new, younger blood in the Republican Party, clearly suggesting herself as that "new blood".

Sanders gifted pundits by posing the choice between crazy or normal when choosing a leader. They had no problem placing Sanders in the former category.

A Party on the Brink

The previous two years had Democrats struggling to pass legislation without cow-towing to the whims of two members of their own party who sought to use the slim Senate majority to gain concessions on certain bills. Because they opposed eliminating the filibuster, Republicans were given a certain degree of leverage they otherwise wouldn't have because they were in the minority.

Now, the tables have turned. Republicans in the House are being forced to submit to the whims of a handful of MAGA representatives. Nowhere was this more obvious than the protracted battle for the speakership, when certain representatives worked out back door deals to gain their support. The slim majority held by Republicans necessitated these evil bargains and showcased the weakness of McCarthy's leadership.

Had the highly anticipated red wave materialized in the midterms, the MAGA faction would have even greater control. They may have even been able to elect one of their own as speaker, further elevating their influence.

Fortunately, the public had grown weary of MAGA politics. Across the board, they refused to support any MAGA candidates not named Trump, giving Republicans a slim majority in the House while Democrats retained control in the Senate, even gaining a seat, which blunted the influence of party pariahs Manchin and Sinema (the latter quickly became an Independent while declaring she would still align herself with the Democrats).

Republicans are at an inflection point. They could continue to go down that long, dark road where conspiracy theories and name-calling become the hallmark of their function in government operations, or they could finally reject MAGA politics and return to being responsible members of a government that works for the people they were elected to represent.

It will take a true red wave to wipe out the scourge that currently threatens to destroy any semblance of what they once. But perhaps wave is the wrong term, maybe a red enema?

◆◆◆

Political Prosecution or Justice Delayed?

By C J Waldron

April 16, 2023

With the unprecedented indictment of Donald Trump, you have a chorus of Republicans crying foul. They are claiming this, and the multiple other legal battles being waged against him, are nothing more than political prosecutions. They are trying to claim that, since Trump is running for his old job in 2024, all investigations should stop while the voters decide whether his actions warrant legal action.

The thing is many of these cases have been on hold as the Department of Justice held to the long-standing policy of not pursuing indictments on a sitting president. It was the primary motivation behind his 2020 run, and the reason he encouraged the January 6th insurrection. Had he won a second term, the statute of limitations would have expired on several pending cases.

It's also the reason he is running again. If he were to win, it could be argued that any current, or future indictments, be put on hold, likely resulting in some of the potential prosecutions being shelved as the clock runs out on the time for charges to be brought.

Republicans want you to believe that, simply by declaring himself a candidate in 2024, all pending cases go into a legal limbo. They claim that doing anything else would amount to giving any potential opponent an unfair advantage because they could use these legal issues as a sign that Trump is unfit for office.

And they would surely know what is and what isn't politically motivated when it comes to legal matters. Their past, and present, actions are evidence of this. They were well aware of Hillary Clinton's political aspirations when they held the Benghazi hearings.

The Whitewater investigation looked into potentially shady real estate dealings by then President Bill Clinton. It morphed into the Monica Lewinsky scandal which ultimately led to his impeachment for lying to Congress about the affair.

Republicans aren't stopping there. They are currently waging a revenge campaign because of the dual Trump impeachments. They are investigating President Biden's son Hunter, who is not in any way involved in any sort of governmental function, in the hope any hint of impropriety will reflect negatively on the president. Yet, they are silent regarding lucrative deals made by White House insiders, and Trump's daughter and son-in-law due to their positions as advisers to the president.

They want Biden investigated regarding the chaotic withdrawal from Afghanistan, but conveniently ignore the fact the wheels to this fiasco were set in motion by the previous administration. That hasn't stopped the lunatic fringe of the party from demanding Biden be impeached, or even that he resign because of this disorganized pull-out.

And then there is the embarrassing Committee to Investigate the Weaponization of the Justice Department. This committee, headed by loudmouth Rep. Jim Jordan, was formed to look into alleged politically motivated investigations, such as the January 6th investigation and the classified documents at Mar a Lago case by claiming they were nothing more than politically motivated witch hunts.

Thus far, this committee has only uncovered wrongdoing by the Trump administration. Other "witnesses" who have been called to testify have made damning, but unsubstantiated, allegations only to be dismissed without the opportunity to be questioned by Democratic members of the committee.

To date Republicans, primarily the poorly named Freedom Caucus, which represents the lunatic fringe of the party, have proposed impeaching President Biden no less than fourteen times. It should come as no surprise that many of these attempts have been proposed by Cruella deVille wannabe Rep. Marjorie Taylor Greene.

Had she been in office at the time there is no doubt Greene would propose articles of impeachment for Barack Obama's tan suit.

When it comes to politically motivated investigations, Republicans certainly know what they are talking about. The problem is, they have it all wrong. Simply declaring you are a candidate should not be a get out of jail free card. It should not put a stop to any ongoing investigations and should definitely not be used as a fundraising tool.

Let the legal system, as slow as it is, decide what is and what isn't a witch hunt. Let justice prevail.

No one is above the law!

◆◆◆

Democracy or Dictatorship? You Choose

By Bob Gatty

Nov. 10, 2023

Donald Trump and his pals are reportedly plotting ways to use the U.S. Justice Department to retaliate against President Biden and his supporters if Trump regains the White House, but voters Tuesday sent another message: Don't count your chickens before they're hatched.

On an election night Nov. 7 with much at stake, Republicans were trounced leading to calls for the firing of GOP Chair Ronna McDaniel. Meanwhile, Trump is making it clear that a repeat term of his presidency would result in revenge and retaliation against his opponents, including former Trump insiders who have turned against him. Such actions would make the U.S. little more than a third-world dictatorship, and Republican leaders seem just fine with that idea.

"This is why Americans needs the RULE OF LAW," wrote former Nixon counsel John W. Dean on X, formerly known as Twitter. "Politics should not be about REVENGE and RETRIBUTION, rather governing a diverse nation of free people. Elect Trump and our democracy ends! His planning for his future presidency is all about a military dictatorship!"

So, democracy or dictatorship? You choose.

Here's what The Washington Post wrote November 7:

"In private, Trump has told advisers and friends in recent months that he wants the Justice Department to investigate onetime officials and allies who have become critical of his time in office, including his former chief of staff, John F. Kelly, and former attorney general William P. Barr, as well as his ex-attorney Ty Cobb and former Joint Chiefs of Staff chairman Gen. Mark A. Milley, according to people who have talked to him, who, like others, spoke on the condition of anonymity to describe private conversations. Trump has also talked of prosecuting officials at the FBI and Justice Department, a person familiar with the matter said.

"In public, Trump has vowed to appoint a special prosecutor to "go after" President Biden and his family. The former president has frequently made corruption accusations against them that are not supported by available evidence."

All of this comes as recent public opinion polling shows Trump leading President Joe Biden in head-to-head matchups, with Biden support softening significantly among young voters and people of color -- polling that has many Democratic supporters and pundits suggesting that Biden should step aside in favor of a younger, more viable candidate.

"I am concerned," Sen. Richard Blumenthal (D-Conn.) told The Washington Post. "I was concerned before these numbers. I am concerned by the inexplicable credibility that Donald Trump seems to have despite all of the indictments, the lies, the incredible wrongdoing."

The Post quoted Cliff Albright, co-founder of the Black Voters Matter Fund, as saying that Biden's support among Black voters in 2020 was less than enthusiastic, but they chose him over Trump as the lesser of two evils.

Albright told The Post that many Black voters, especially younger ones, have been disillusioned by Biden's policies, especially on student debt — his effort to forgive borrowers was overturned by the Supreme Court — and his fervent support of Israel. Albright said he expects many Black voters to still support Biden, but that Biden needs to do some work to keep them in the fold.

If what Albright says is true about young Black voters being pissed because Biden has not succeeded in rolling back their student loans, that is incredible. What do they expect him to do when the Supreme Court ruled against his plan? Do they not remember that the Court is now dominated by Trump's appointed justices? Even with that ruling, Biden has tried via executive orders to reduce economic hardships caused by student debt. He deserves credit for that effort.

The Stench of Mitch McConnell

Election night November 7, however, provided Democrats with some good news, and results in many states, including conservative Ohio, gave them reason for optimism and ammunition for success next November.

Despite Biden's apparent unpopularity (largely because of his age, I suspect), Democrats won crucial victories. Kentucky voters easily re-elected **Democratic** Gov. Andy Beshear, putting him in the conversation as a potential presidential candidate. In fact, Beshear's victory over Trump's chosen candidate, state Attorney General Daniel Cameron, prompted Trump to blame Cameron's loss (he once had a 25-point lead) on Senate Minority Leader Mitch McConnell (R-Ky).

"Daniel Cameron lost because he couldn't alleviate the stench of Mitch McConnell," Trump wrote on Truth Social. "I told him early that's a big burden to overcome. McConnell and [Utah Senator Mitch] Romney are Kryptonite for Republican Candidates."

In Pennsylvania, Democrat Daniel McCaffery won an open seat on the state Supreme Court; and in Virginia, Democrats maintained their state Senate majority and recaptured the House of Delegates. That likely dooms Gov. Glenn Youngkin's hopes for curbing abortion rights, and most likely any hopes he might have of running for president if Trump fails.

In fact, Democrats opposing Republican efforts to restrict abortions did well. In ruby red Ohio, voters approved by a margin of 56.6 to 43.4 percent an amendment adding abortion rights to the state constitution. Clearly, the Supreme Court's overturning of *Roe v. Wade* last year is motivating voters, and Democrats are capitalizing on that.

"Voters came out in droves to send a clear message: Ohioans believe women's health care decisions should be between them and their doctors, not politicians," said Sen. Sherrod Brown (D-Ohio) at the top of a fundraising email distributed Wednesday.

Key Election Results

Here's a summary of the Nov. 7 election results as provided by the Biden-Harris campaign:

Abortion was considered "the running theme of the night" as Republicans were "dogged by abortion positions to the right of the electorate, even in red states."

In Ohio, despite Republicans' best efforts to mislead voters and distract from the issues on the ballot, Ohioans decisively voted to protect repro-

41

ductive rights. It's the seventh state since 2022 where abortion access has been on the ballot directly – and every single time voters have overwhelmingly voted in favor of reproductive freedoms.

In Kentucky, which Trump won by 26 points in 2020, voters rejected Cameron's support for the commonwealth's abortion ban that has no exceptions for rape and incest, sending Andy Beshear back to the Governor's mansion.

In Virginia, where Youngkin spent nearly $15 million to try to take total control of the Virginia government to pass an abortion ban, Virginians soundly rejected his efforts, holding the state Senate and flipping the House of Delegates into Democratic control.

In Pennsylvania, voters across the commonwealth blocked Republican Carolyn Carluccio – who was endorsed by extreme anti-abortion groups – from the Pennsylvania Supreme Court and elected Democrat Daniel Mc-Caffery to safeguard reproductive rights.

Voters rejected Republicans' dangerous anti-democracy agenda:

In Pennsylvania, voters rejected Carolyn Carluccio – the Republican candidate for Supreme Court who refused to say who won the 2020 election – in support of Democrat Daniel McCaffery who campaigned on protecting voting rights.

In Kentucky, Cameron, who refused to denounce Donald Trump's dangerous election denials, significantly underperformed candidates who strongly rejected stolen election conspiracies.

Voters rejected Republicans' MAGAnomics agenda:

In Virginia, Youngkin and MAGA Republicans relentlessly campaigned on giving tax breaks to the wealthy – and lost.

In Kentucky, Republicans spent $30 million focused on attacking Joe Biden in an attempt to defeat Governor Beshear – they even attacked him for supporting Bidenomics. It didn't work.

Cameron closed his campaign for Kentucky governor with Donald Trump campaigning for him – and he lost. President Biden and Vice President Harris endorsed 23 Democratic state legislature candidates **in Virginia** – two-thirds of them won.

The Biden-Harris coalition is energized – and they're turning out to vote:

In Pennsylvania, the number of absentee ballot returns for youth voters statewide more than doubled since 2021, campus precincts saw substantial increases in student turnout compared to 2021, and Philadelphia County far surpassed 2021 turnout

In Ohio, more than 70% of Hispanic voters and more than 80% of Black voters and voters under 30 years old voted to protect reproductive rights.

Republicans had **"a turnout/enthusiasm problem"** even in states like deep red Kentucky.

Many a Slip 'Twixt the Cup and the Lip

So, what does all this mean? Are these polls showing Trump ahead of Biden fully a year out from next year's election a cause for concern?

During this coming year we will learn if Trump continues to be a viable candidate considering his indictments, trials, and the clear possibility that he could be convicted and even sent to prison. What will Republicans do then? Who will they turn to?

Who's old?

And remember, Trump is only three years younger than Biden, who will be 81 on Nov. 20, but as fat as he is, he appears to be in much worse physical condition than the president. So, if voters buy into the GOP messaging that Biden is unhealthy and too old, that really doesn't wash when compared to Trump, despite Trump's makeup which is supposed to make him appear younger.

Meanwhile, Biden's achievements have been remarkable, and he continues to do his job, and he does it well. And he is unalterably committed to preserving and defending our democracy.

Trump? Do you really want to turn our country over to a twice impeached, four-times indicted ego maniac who is determined to exact retribution against his perceived enemies and use the power of the government to exact revenge?

The bottom line is this: Do you want to continue to live in a Democracy or in a dictatorship?

Again, Republicans on the far right are attempting to tie any aid to Israel to enhanced border security.

So, once again. Democracy or dictatorship? You choose.

◆◆◆

The Great American Divide Continues

By C J Waldron

Nov. 25, 2023

It's no great secret that America is a highly polarized nation. Many times, the split is along party lines, but there are also divisions within each party that threaten to tear the country apart. This schism within parties has resulted in an inability to effectively govern, and the world is noticing.

In the Democratic Party, you have the moderates battling the progressives over the direction their members should take. Moderates want a traditional approach, with social programs and infrastructure taking the lead while Progressives are demanding more aggressive action when it comes to battling Climate Change, which is the key issue on their agenda.

On the other side of the aisle are the Republicans, who find themselves divided into three factions. First, there are the old-school Conservatives who still believe bipartisan legislation is possible under certain circumstances. Then there are the hardliners of the Freedom Caucus, who will only agree to possible legislation if specific demands are met. And finally, there is the MAGA wing that only wants to prevent anything from happening until Donald Trump is reinstated in the Oval Office.

Each side also has individual members who have stymied the legislative process. Former football coach turned professional obstructionist, Tommy Tuberville, has defied even members of his own party by single-handedly blocking any military promotions until his demand to restrict reproductive rights is met.

On the Democratic side, the not-soon-enough-to-be-retired Joe Manchin has caused unnecessary delays as he forced watered-down versions of the Infrastructure Law and Economic Recovery Act through Congress over his demand that certain emissions standards be weakened to appease his coal miner constituents. Rather than offer to retrain miners to work in developing cleaner alternatives, he is cow-towing to the coal mining executives who have largely financed his congressional tenure.

As the 2024 presidential election draws closer, Republicans are generally united in returning Donald Trump to the White House despite his continuing rhetoric that he will be an authoritarian ruler, ignoring the will of others in his party if his needs aren't met.

Meanwhile, Democrats are ambivalent in their support of President Biden's re-election bid. While many cite his age, others are worried he won't have the backing of the voters when it comes to defeating Trump. Recent polls have shown that to be a legitimate concern, but these same polls had Hillary Clinton winning in 2016, so they can't be taken as being accurate.

There are many issues causing the great American divide that threatens to tear the very fabric of our democracy to shreds.

The Wars in Israel and Ukraine

While no American soldiers are actively engaged in the wars in Ukraine or the battle between Hamas and Israel, at least not in an official capacity, there is still intense debate over our contributions to both conflicts. In Ukraine, the American government has spent or proposed $75 billion in arms and other assistance.

Under an arrangement with President Obama, Israel receives $3.8 billion in annual military assistance. President Biden is proposing an additional $2 billion to aid in their current war with Hamas.

While there was near-unanimous support for funding the effort to thwart Russian aggression in Ukraine at the outset, hardliners on the far right are now opposing any further attempt to prevent the absorption of Ukraine into Russia, as it was during the days of the former Soviet Union.

Meanwhile, conservative Republicans, even their Minority Leader in the Senate, who was once derided as being "Moscow Mitch" for his apparent support for Vladimir Putin, have pledged to support further aid to Ukraine. They view Ukraine as Putin's first step in reclaiming nations that were once part of the Soviet Union. If he is allowed to go unchallenged, Putin would feel emboldened to attempt to annex these other countries.

The hardliners on the right, mainly comprised of supporters of Donald Trump, are starting to erect roadblocks to further Ukrainian aid. They have refused to support funding to keep the government operating if it includes such aid. They have demanded that any future funding also include specific anti-immigration measures. And they believe Trump's boast that, if re-elected, he would immediately end the war in Ukraine, presumably by capitulating to Putin's demands.

Regarding the situation in Israel, there was a strong show of bipartisan support following the heinous, unprovoked attacks by Hamas on October 7th. This rare show of unity quickly unraveled as Israel launched a retaliatory campaign against Hamas with innocent Palestinian civilians left caught in the crossfire. This has led to intraparty squabbles and a sharp rise in both anti-Semitic and anti-Muslim attacks.

Even funding for Donald Trump's boondoggle of a border wall. They have threatened to oppose any such assistance to Israel that doesn't include these provisions.

And the beat goes on.

◆ ◆ ◆

The Dangerous Reality of Sleepwalking into a Dictatorship

By Bob Gatty

Dec. 3, 2023

Donald Trump is warning Americans that if he is sent back to the White House, he will use the power of the federal government against those who have opposed him, essentially turning the Justice Department into his own, personal police force.

Former GOP U.S. Rep. Liz Cheney, whose father, Dick Cheney, was vice president under President George W. Bush and a hardline Republican, is now warning that voters should listen to Trump's pledge, that it's not simply hyperbole being spewed by the orange creature.

"He's told us what he will do," Cheney said on CBS. "It's very easy to see the steps that he will take. … People who say, 'Well, if he's elected, it's not that dangerous because we have all of these checks and balances,' don't fully understand the extent to which the Republicans in Congress today have been co-opted. … One of the things that we see happening today is a sort of a sleepwalking into dictatorship in the United States."

Cheney, who maintains her solid conservative credentials, also warned that new House Speaker Mike Johnson (R-LA) is in cahoots with Trump and will support those efforts of retribution by the defeated, twice impeached, and four-times indicted former president.

"If you look at what Donald Trump is trying to do, he can't do it by himself," Cheney told CBS Correspondent John Dickerson in an interview. "He has to have collaborators. And the story of Mike Johnson is a story of, of a collaborator and of someone who knew then – and knows now – that what he's doing and saying is wrong, but he's willing to do it in an effort to please Donald Trump. And that's what makes it dangerous."

Johnson already is doing Trump's bidding, going after President Joe Biden with a phony impeachment inquiry that is based on nothing except hate and retribution. Appearing on Fox News with Rep. Elise Stefanik (R-NY), another Trump loyalist, Johnson said he intends to bring a vote on impeachment.

"Elise and I both served on the impeachment defense team of Donald Trump twice, when the Democrats used it for brazen, partisan political purposes. We decried that use of it," said Johnson. "This is very different. Remember, we are the rule-of-law team. We have to do it very methodically," he said.

That is hilarious! The Republicans, who blindly support an ego maniac who tried to overthrow the 2020 election among other criminal acts including violating the Espionage Act and fraudulent business dealings, claim to be the "law and order team?" What a joke!

The Republicans, of course, are using questions about Biden's son, Hunter, and his business activities to tarnish the president, and last month issued subpoenas asking Hunter, the president's brother, James, and family associate Rob Walker to appear for depositions. Hunter said he would testify publicly before the House Oversight Committee, but the Republicans said, 'oh no, we want this done behind closed doors."

Really? What are they afraid of?

Obviously, the MAGA Republicans who now effectively control the House of Representatives, want to do everything possible to discredit Biden, hoping desperately to return Trump to the presidency because that could be the only way for him to escape being sent to federal prison.

In fact, Steven Sadow, Trump's lead counsel in the Fulton County, GA racketeering case against Trump, told the judge Dec. 1 that if Trump wins the 2024 election, his trial on charges that he conspired to overturn his election loss in Georgia would have to wait until after he leaves the White House.

Meanwhile, Trump continues to tell us exactly what he would do if elected -- like use the power of the federal government to attack his opponents and kill off the Affordable Care Act, something he and the Republicans already attempted, but failed. You have to wonder why would he drag up an issue that already has been settled, one that few people support? It makes no sense.

Like everything else about Trump and the Republicans, it's all about lies, misrepresentations, and threats, as this graphic pulled from Facebook indicates.

Incredibly, Trump now is trying to claim support from Black Lives Matter, a movement that he has derided in the past. In a post on Truth Social, Trump called Rhode Island BLM activist Mark Fisher "a great guy" and said he was "very honored to have his and BLM's support."

Only problem is that it's just another Trump exaggeration (i.e., lie) as a spokesperson for the Rhode Island BLM group disclosed that Fisher is no longer affiliated with them.

So, the lies, threats, exaggerations keep coming and the MAGA crowd swallows it all up. Are they ready for a Trump dictatorship?

◆◆◆

2024: The Rematch No-one Wants

By C J Waldron

Jan 21, 2024

Americans are faced with the prospect of a 2024 Presidential race that promises to be a rematch of the ugly 2020 contest. While most Americans enjoy a good rematch, (think Ali/Frazier), the potential battle for the highest office in the land has many souring on politics that have become too ugly and too divisive.

Because it's the rematch no-one wants, the end result may be that many voters will choose to sit this one out, setting up the possibility that a minority of the population will be the ultimate deciders in whatever future our country will see.

The Age Factor

Despite many Democrats expressing respect for President Biden, a large number say they won't support a second term due to his age. While most won't say it directly, the implication is that he is experiencing a cognitive decline because of his advanced age. They worry that this could quickly accelerate, leaving him unable to effectively carry out the duties of the Office of President.

Those on the right are only too willing to exploit this perception. They pounce on any verbal gaffe or physical misstep, citing them as proof of Biden's cognitive decline. They intimate that pauses in his speaking patterns are proof of his mental deterioration despite it being widely known that Biden is a life-long stutterer, and these hesitations are a consequence of that condition.

Yet, when it comes to Donald Trump, they are willing to overlook his verbal gaffes. They regularly accept his lies as facts as he releases phantom medical diagnoses and declares he has "aced" a cognitive test that is actually meant to detect signs of dementia. (It makes you wonder why his doctors decided he needed such an assessment in the first place).

The age factor will certainly be an important issue in the 2024 election. The problem is that it is not being assessed equally.

The Economic Disconnect

Wages are up; inflation and unemployment are down. Yet many Americans don't believe President Biden has effectively handled the economy. Of his recent poll numbers, Biden scores the lowest on this issue despite months of positive indications about the state of the economy.

So, what's behind the disconnect between the facts and the sour mood many Americans have about the economy?

The pandemic caused a great deal of economic upheaval as businesses were forced to scale back and even shut down due to COVID restrictions. Yet, for many, there was a silver lining amidst the economic upheaval. Pandemic relief funds and a moratorium on evictions saw many Americans with positive bank balances for the first time in their lives.

When the nation re-opened, Americans went on a spending spree with their newfound wealth. This rapid increase in demand led to inevitable supply chain issues resulting in surging prices and higher inflation.

Of course, many blamed President Biden for these problems. They saw soaring gas prices as a result of Biden's economic policies and not a dramatic increase in demand as manufacturers tried to meet these overwhelming requests. They viewed supply chain issues as the Biden administration's inability to effectively handle the economy.

Many economists even predicted that the US was headed toward an inevitable recession because of the economic problems the pandemic created. But the recession didn't happen. Prices eased. Soaring gas prices came down. Inflation and unemployment numbers plummeted. The American economy was back on its feet.

So, why do many Americans believe Biden has done a poor job of handling the economy?

The disconnect may lie in the fact many benefitted from the pandemic assistance and not having to pay rent or mortgages for several months. They enjoyed their post-pandemic spending spree despite the higher prices and limited availability. When these advantages were no longer an option, they sought a scapegoat. And of course, many blamed President Biden.

Like he did in 2020, Donald Trump is predicting that America is headed for a major recession should Biden win in 2024. He is claiming that Biden's economic success is only due to programs enacted during his administration. This ignores that the economy cratered, largely because of the pandemic, during his time in office. He also fails to admit that his own positive numbers regarding the economy were largely the result of policies enacted by his predecessor, President Obama.

President Biden was able to pass the Inflation Reduction Act, which is a huge benefit to many struggling Americans. Contrast that to Trump's so-called Tax Relief package which was mainly a boon to wealthy Americans.

Trump spent his entire time in office touting the need to address the country's ailing infrastructure. Yet, he was never able to whip up enough support to get anything done about it. President Biden made this a priority and was able to get an Infrastructure Bill passed very quickly.

His reelection campaign has tried, and failed, to make "Bidenomics" a central issue. Yet many Americans still doubt his ability to effectively handle the economy.

Why this has remained a mystery.

Voting Restrictions and Abortion

Republicans are trying to shape the upcoming election as a referendum on abortion. This is despite the fact that a majority of Americans support a woman's right to choose. It is a nod to the Christian Nationalist wing of the party that has, with the selection of Mike Johnson as Speaker of the House, taken hold of the Republican agenda in the House of Representatives. They have reduced the complex, emotional decision to terminate a pregnancy to a trite bumper sticker: "Abortion is Murder".

Women who try to terminate a pregnancy, even for legitimate health reasons, are being treated as criminals. A thirty-three year old Black woman from Ohio was charged with abuse of a corpse after she suffered a miscarriage. The post-Roe world is forcing women to take drastic measures to protect their health because they are being denied access to an abortion, even if the fetus isn't viable or the life of the mother is at risk.

These same religious hypocrites are claiming a "God-given right" to bear arms as they clutch a Bible in one hand and an assault rifle in the other. Yet they claim they want to preserve the sanctity of life while these same weapons are being used to murder children.

The potential candidates have staked their claim on the issue of abortion...sort of. Joe Biden is a devout Catholic, and his church is firmly opposed to any type of abortion, even in cases of rape, incest or where the life of the mother is at risk. Despite his religious beliefs, Biden has sworn to bow to the will of the people. With a majority of the country supporting a woman's right to choose, he has defended this, even in the face of having Catholic priests denying him communion.

And then there is Donald Trump who has repeatedly flip-flopped on the issue, depending on his contrary mood swings. Prior to his entrance into the political arena, he was pro-choice. It had even been alleged that he paid for a woman to terminate her pregnancy and attributed it to his doorman, but if rumors are true, and this certainly goes against his refusal to pay for anything, it was actually *his* unborn child that he paid to have aborted.

Fast forward to today and Trump is boasting to have personally over-turned Roe by virtue of appointing three justices to the Supreme Court. It's highly unlikely that Trump elevated this trio of Conservatives as a way to over-turn the landmark decision. Instead, it's more likely that Trump, being one who always views things on a transactional basis, put them on the bench with the belief that they would consistently rule in his favor out of loyalty.

Fortunately, this has proven to be a false hope. Other than Clarence Thomas, who was not a Trump appointee, the court has ruled against him, es-pecially in cases involving overturning the 2020 election. That hasn't stopped Trump from appealing to the Supreme Court in an effort to delay the multiple court cases he has on his crowded calendar.

Democrats are hoping the issue of abortion will counter Republicans' screams about border security. At this point, they are demanding that any issue, even those supporting Israel and Ukraine, be tied to enhanced anti-im-migration measures. This is alienating the Progressive wing of the Democratic Party, which has already expressed hesitation over supporting Biden due to his age.

The Silent Majority

When Richard Nixon was being attacked, even by members of his own party, he claimed to have the support of a "Silent Majority" who continued to support him. Fast forward to today and you have the opposite situation occurring. Donald Trump appears to have widespread support among Republicans. Yet, this could all be an illusion. Many can be putting up a front, feigning support, while they privately will make another choice when it comes to actually casting their vote.

They have witnessed what happens to those who back another can-didate and are falsely claiming they will vote for Trump when they enter the voting booth. That could result in another candidate emerging as the favored nominee when the choice is made during their national convention.

The problem with this is that Trump will almost definitely mount a third-party challenge. He is acutely aware that any chance of his avoiding the consequences of his actions is to retake the Oval Office and issue himself a presidential pardon. While this won't protect him from the cases in Georgia and New York, he can use his position to delay these cases.

On the other hand, Joe Biden may need a Silent Majority to step forward if he is to win re-election. His approval ratings are currently underwater as Muslims are saying they won't support him due to his handling of the situation in Israel, and young voters are vowing to withhold their support over Biden's handling of the environment, abortion and student loan forgiveness.

People of Color are upset over Biden's inability to protect their right to vote and systemic racism in law enforcement. They are also those who have yet to reap the benefits of Biden's economic agenda as their unemployment numbers continue to lag behind the rest of the nation.

If any, or all of these groups fails to support President Biden, or if they choose not to vote at all, it will seal Biden's defeat.

The Clock is Ticking

As we begin 2024, the clock is ticking on so many fronts. There are the primaries, which seem to be an exercise in futility, since both parties seem set on their choices, whether anyone likes it or not. There are at least four criminal proceedings where Donald Trump is racing the clock in hopes he can delay any or all of the four trials he is currently facing. Trump is trying to get the Supreme Court to slow walk its decision on his federal trial regarding the events surrounding January 6th. He is hoping to retake the White House and then declare a halt to the proceedings.

Recent polling indicates that up to a quarter of his supporters will not vote to re-elect him if Trump is convicted in any of these cases. This gives him further motivation to delay the proceedings until after election day. Trump's attorneys are attempting to make the same argument before the Supreme Court, that he has absolute immunity, that failed in his effort to have charges dismissed.

If Trump is successful in getting his trials delayed until after Election Day, there is the possibility that he could be convicted between November and January 20th. There are no restrictions in the Constitution that prohibit a convicted felon from serving as president, yet he would likely pardon himself on the Federal charges.

That leaves Georgia. Trump's lawyers have been unsuccessful in getting the case moved to Federal Court so Trump could pardon himself. A Georgia conviction could have Trump facing real jail time. Trump would undoubtedly want his sentence held in abeyance until his term ends. But he has already suggested that he would wield dictatorial power, meaning he would remain in office for life.

On the other side, despite being the incumbent, Joe Biden is facing low approval ratings. If it was only based upon one issue it might be easier to address. But Democrats seem hell-bent on opposing his re-election because they have an axe to grind on a single topic.

Younger voters complain he hasn't done enough to protect the environment, while they ignore that Donald Trump is once again threatening to withdraw from the Paris Climate Agreement. Muslims are saying they will abandon Biden for his lack of action in supporting a ceasefire in Gaza while they turn a deaf ear to Trump's promise to re-institute a Muslim ban. Jews are saying they won't support Biden because he hasn't done enough to address the rise in antisemitic attacks despite the fact these are coming from the Right. Progressives are attacking his age while offering no younger alternative.

And those are just within his own party.

MAGA Republicans in the House have launched their own attacks with a sham impeachment investigation that has yielded zero results. The main impact is that they can claim that, despite Trump being impeached twice, Biden is also facing similar punishment.

Election season is upon us. Trump can claim a "resounding victory" in the Iowa Caucus but, as Mark Twain once said, "There are lies, there are damned lies and there are statistics." While he outdistanced his opponents by 30%, it was only 110,000 out of a possible 3 million registered voters, so to declare it a mandate would certainly be a stretch.

Even so, Trump was only able to garner 51% of the vote, meaning almost half of those who opted to brave the frigid temperatures thought another candidate would be better suited to take on President Biden in the Fall. This obvious weakness has other candidates pouncing in hopes of becoming the Republican nominee.

At a recent Town Hall, Nikki Haley depicted the potential rematch as "two 80-year-olds running for president while the country is in disarray". She failed to mention that much of the disarray is the result of her own party's doing. Instead, she tried to paint both Trump and Biden as equally responsible while offering herself as a younger alternative that would allow the nation to move on from the current political divisions.

Yet, even if Haley wins in New Hampshire and other states, she may not win the nomination. Trump-friendly delegates have vowed to support his ascension even if he loses the primaries. In other words, they want to ignore the will of the voters in favor of loyalty to the MAGA cult.

Haley, along with Ron DeSantis, the only other candidates still in the race, is largely ignoring Trump's biggest liability. Both refuse to bring up his criminal prosecution and his responsibility for the January 6th insurrection. Instead, they attack each other while vaguely referencing Trump's multiple comments about being a dictator and a path of vengeance he threatens to unleash should he win re-election.

Catching Fire and Mental Health

Being an incumbent usually has the advantage of constantly being on the national stage. So far, the Biden administration has failed to capitalize on this. There is no catchphrase, such as "Morning in America" or "Hope and

Change" that has resonated with the voters. "Bidenomics" has fallen flat due to many Americans failing to reap the benefits of a booming economy. And, as of yet, there is no unifying message to propel Biden into the spotlight.

Meanwhile, Trump has had years to hone his MAGA messaging. His multiple legal woes are being decried as "Witch Hunts", politically persecution and election interference, even as his supporters in Congress are conducting sham impeachment inquiries and demanding prosecutors turn over evidence related to Trump's indictments, which is a clear case of obstruction of justice.

Trump supporters are quick to jump on any Biden misstep or verbal gaffe, yet conveniently ignore Trump's own mental decline. They gloss over his declaration to become a dictator. They turn a blind eye to his confusing Presidents Biden and Obama. They disregard his comments on a supposed test of his mental acuity when the evaluation is actually meant to detect signs of dementia.

It's all part of the MAGA narrative. And if we aren't careful, it may be successful.

The Rematch No-one Wants

All signs point to a likely rematch of the 2020 election. Trump supporters are out to prove that the election was a fluke, which would also reinforce their claims that the election was rigged. Biden supporters are out to preserve Democracy in the face of authoritarian threats.

The election has dire consequences for the future of America, and the world at large. Vote Blue!

◆◆◆

Contraception? Just 'Put it Between Your Knees', Ladies

By Bob Gatty

March 11, 2024

In the latest Republican sexist attack on women's rights, Arizona Senate Majority Leader Sonny Borrelli, who opposes legislation guaranteeing the right to contraceptives, says women can avoid getting pregnant simply by keeping their legs closed.

"Like I said, Bayer Company invented aspirin," said Borrelli, who spent a day in jail on domestic violence charges in 2001. "Put it between your knees."

In other words, women wouldn't need birth control if they kept a pill bottle between their legs to prevent having sex. His sexist comments came as Republicans continue to stall legislation sought by Gov. Katie Hobbs that would assure access to contraception in the state.

Clearly, Borrelli learned nothing from that experience 23 years ago when he pled guilty to a "class 1 misdemeanor disorderly conduct charge tagged with domestic violence." His then-wife's child told police he saw his dad rapidly punch his mother three times in the mouth before shoving her to the ground. Borrelli later said his then-wife had experienced a "meltdown" and "psychotic episode", and that her injuries were self-inflicted. He said he took the guilty plea to avoid losing custody of his son -- the one who ratted him out.

MAGA devotee Borrelli fits right in with the misogynistic Donald Trump, whom he supported following the January 6, 2021, Trump-inspired attack on the U.S. Capitol intended to prevent certification of Joe Biden's election. In fact, there were calls that he and six other Arizona lawmakers should be kicked out of the state legislature for supporting Trump's "Stop the Steal" initiative that led to that attack.

"This sexist tirade is just the latest in Republicans' far-ranging attacks on women and their access to reproductive care across the country. From undermining access to contraceptives to attacking IVF services to banning abortion, reproductive freedom is the top target of MAGA extremism," declared a news release issued by the Democratic Legislative Campaign Committee (DLCC).

"A comment like this from the Arizona Senate majority leader is indicative of just how far extreme Republicans have taken us and how little the GOP values women in this state," said Arizona DLCC co-chair Sen. Priya Sundareshan. "There are consequences when our elected officials are this extreme. As long as Arizona Republicans are in power, our reproductive freedoms are deeply threatened. For the sake of our families' futures, we must elect Democrats who will protect our most basic freedoms."

"It's disgusting that comments like 'put it between your knees' are being voiced by elected leaders in 2024," declared DLCC National Press Secretary Sam Paisley. "It's even more upsetting that this comment is accompanied by Republican obstruction of legislation that would protect contraception access in Arizona. Misogyny is clearly alive and well at the highest levels of the Arizona Republican Party.

"Sen. Borrelli's words and actions aren't happening in a void – he's unfortunately emblematic of the extremism of Republicans across the country," said Paisley. "State legislatures are the most important level of the ballot deciding reproductive freedom, and the DLCC is all hands-on deck to root out MAGA extremism and elect Democrats who will defend reproductive rights – including in both chambers of the Arizona legislature. Arizona Republicans have been put on notice: they will answer for their extremism at the polls in November."

Borrelli's comments echo those made by late Wisconsin pastor and former GOP mega donor Foster Freiss. In 2012, while Freiss was the head of a super PAC that backed Republican presidential candidate Rick Santorum, Freiss said women putting aspirin between their knees would be a cheaper alternative to contraception.

Late last month, in denouncing the Alabama Supreme Court's ruling on in vitro fertilization, Rep. Alexandria Ocasio-Cortez (D-NY) tied the ban to the misogyny being embraced within the conservative movement.

Essentially, the ruling classifies frozen embryos as people under Alabama law and prohibits embryos from being discarded, even if the embryo is not to be implanted. Paired with the conservative movement's ongoing attack on contraception, the IVF ruling highlights what Ocasio-Cortez described as "a patriarchal theocracy" that's gaining ground in the conservative movement.

The movement's endgame, according to Ocasio-Cortez, is to deny women their sexual freedom by ensuring that sex is used primarily for pregnancy, rather than pleasure.

Ocasio-Cortez told MSNBC, "I want to be very clear that this was intentional and that this is exactly what Republicans have been going for. We've seen it. You have the Heritage Foundation, you have lots of folks who are on record saying, you know, not only do they want to go after abortion, not only do they want to go after reproductive freedom, they're going after IVF. They're going after contraception. We have a mifepristone ruling that is coming down from the Supreme Court and Clarence Thomas enriching himself from the same folks who are saying that they are trying to control women's bodies quite explicitly. And going beyond that, they also want to control what they call 'recreational sex.'"

Ocasio-Cortez was referring to the Supreme Court's scheduled hearing on mifepristone, the commonly used abortion pill, in a case brought by the conservative Alliance for Hippocratic Medicine. That hearing will take place March 26.

Tell me again why anyone in their right mind would be a Republican, and why would any woman -- ANY woman -- support them.

◆◆◆

Sorry, Judge, I Just Can't Pay

By Bob Gatty

March 18, 2024

Since when can you simply tell a judge in a case where you've been fined even $1,000 that you simply don't have the money to pay, so he should cut you some slack?

Apparently, that's what Donald Trump is trying to do with the $450 million judgement levied against him in the New York business fraud case, as he's asked the appellate court for a reprieve, so the state won't seize his assets, like his famed Trump Tower in Manhattan.

Is it any wonder that he can't find an insurer to finance his appeal bond to cover that judgement? Why would they do that with Trump's reputation for stiffing his creditors? We're talking about $450 million here. That's not chicken feed.

In a filing with the Appellate Division of the New York Supreme Court, Trump's lawyers said that Trump and the Trump Organization have struck out in their efforts to find an insurer that would accept property as collateral, apparently meaning that Trump -- who has claimed to be worth billions -- doesn't have the cash to cover the judgement.

Time is running out, too, as the bond is due to be posted within a week, and Trump's request that the judge accept a $100 million bond instead of the total $450 million was rejected. As an aside, what would happen if you owed the feds $4,500 in taxes and you asked them to take $1,000 instead. I'm sure that would work.

Sorry Judge, I Just Can't Pay

According to Alan Garten, the Trump Organization's general counsel, they approached some 30 surety bond providers, and none would accept real estate as collateral for the bond.

We'll see how this plays out, but some knowledgeable observers suggest that this could be the beginning of the unraveling of the Trump empire. How long will it be before Trump's assets are seized by the court to cover that judgement, which, by the way, grows larger due to accumulating interest every hour of every day that it goes unpaid?

Where will Trump get the dough to cover that judgement? At $400 a pair, he would have to sell more than 112,000 pairs of his golden Trump sneakers to generate $450 million -- and that's not subtracting whatever the production costs are for those nasty looking shoes.

In fact, more than $450 million is needed since the surety companies are requiring Trump to put up the entire amount needed, or about $464 million, according to the defense filing. *The Washington Post* reported that legal experts say the key reason companies refuse to help Trump is that they don't think his appeal will succeed.

What does all of this mean for Trump's presidential bid? How can he come down the golden escalator like he did in 2016 when he kicked off his campaign -- if he no longer owns Trump Tower?

Will he turn to his donors, those fools who buy into his false promises and outright lies, to get him out of the hole? That's already happening.

A woman by the name of Elena Cardone previously organized a fundraiser for her embattled hero and reportedly has raised more than $1.3 million of a $355 million goal, which, by the way, is more than $100 million less than what Trump needs.

Her explanation for her appeal states in part:

"I am a wife of Grant Cardone, mother and an ardent supporter of American values and an advocate for justice, I stand unwaveringly with President Donald Trump in the face of what I see as unprecedented and unfair treatment by certain judicial elements in New York.

"The recent legal battles he faces are not just an attack on him, but an attack on the very ideals of fairness and due process that every American deserves. It's a moment that calls into question the balance of justice and the application of law, disproportionately aimed at silencing a voice that has been at the forefront of advocating for American strength, prosperity, and security."

"This fundraiser, therefore, is not merely about raising the "ruling" amount. It's about making a stand. It's about showing that when one of us is targeted for championing the values that make America great, he does not stand alone. We stand with him, shoulder to shoulder, ready to support, defend, and fight back against a system that threatens to undermine the very foundations of our republic."

It is incredible how Trump has fooled people into believing his lies. As this is written, donations to Cardone's Go Fund Me Trump campaign continue to roll in. "Anonymous" contributed $10K, the top donation. But others are chipping in -- $5,000 each from Kenneth McKelvey, Nicholas Minassi, Anonymous, and Aaron Jones. Then, there's $3,500 from Derek Murray, $3,000 from Ronald Jackson, and $2,500 from another "anonymous" donor. Then there are many small contributors, people contributing just $10 or $20.

Suckers, all.

Cardone says she's "an ardent supporter of American values and an advocate for justice." If that's the case, why would she ever go out of her way to help Trump? The only values he supports are those that will line his pockets and keep him out of jail.

◆ ◆ ◆

A Rapist in the White House?

By C J Waldron

May 8, 2024

Listening to her testimony in what the media is inaccurately calling the "Hush Money Trial" it is difficult to escape the question of whether Donald Trump used his position of power to rape Stormy Daniels.

In her sworn testimony, she details how he used his physical stature, along with dangling an offer to appear on his popular television show, to force himself upon the then 27-year-old adult film actress.

While the story of the 2007 encounter has been out there for some time, the sordid details were missing. Indeed, Trump's defense team went to great lengths to exclude as much of the incident as possible with numerous objections. Trump was reported to have hit his attorneys on the arm in order to get them to object to damning or embarrassing testimony.

The judge in the case has tried to curtail the sexual aspects of Stephanie Clifford's (AKA Stormy Daniels) testimony since the true focus of the allegations is related to fraudulent business practices. However, the information being revealed is certainly relevant, especially when it is connected to the infamous *Access Hollywood* video.

Even as the judge has recommended that the prosecution move along, the phrase from Trump's *Access Hollywood* tape, "I moved on her like a bitch," certainly mirrors the events of his encounter with Daniels. Daniels describes "blacking out," which is common when dealing with a traumatic experience, when she emerged from the bathroom to find Trump on the bed dressed in only boxers and a t-shirt. She said that she felt as if she was drugged but denied that she actually was.

Her testimony described a brief sexual encounter and how she rushed to exit after it was over. She testified that she related the incident to several friends, but only described the sexual aspects to a few close friends. She also described how future encounters with Trump, who would later demean Daniels by calling her "Horseface", where he tried to initiate another sexual liaison.

The power dynamic Trump used in what his attorneys are calling a "consensual encounter" is al, too familiar. Disgraced Hollywood producer Harvey Weinstein has been convicted for using such tactics to force himself onto many unsuspecting actresses. The *Access Hollywood* tape and Trump's recent civil conviction are strong indicators that he used the same maneuvers to force himself on Stormy Daniels.

Like many rape victims, Daniels denies she was sexually assaulted. And while the statute of limitations has likely run out, there is still the specter of whether or not there will be a rapist in the White House in 2025.

◆◆◆

What Crime? Today Trump Got the Answer

By Bob Gatty

May 30, 2024

Two days ago, here in ruby red Myrtle Beach, SC, I was behind a big black pickup truck with five huge American flags mounted in the back and big, bold "Let's Go Brandon" signs emblazoned on the lift gate, doors, and fenders.

I pulled up next to the driver, tapped my horn to get his attention, and wait for it…gave him the finger. He rolled down the passenger side window and yelled an obscenity, to which I responded with "I can't believe you're still supporting a criminal to be president."

"What crime did he commit?" the MAGAT yelled back. "What crime?"

Today came the answer as Trump was found guilty by a New York jury on all 34 felony charges that he faced in connection with the $130,000 hush money payment that he made through fixer Michael Cohen to former porn star Stormy Daniels to keep her quiet about an alleged 2006 sexual encounter, which Trump denies.

Wish I could find that guy with the truck now.

"Hey pal, you got your answer," I would tell him. "He's a convicted felon. Still gonna vote for him? Maybe you should take that crap off your truck."

Although that MAGAT lives in my neighborhood, I'm not going to go looking for him. South Carolina loves guns, and people die from road rage here. Still, I wonder what this guy's thinking now. "Rigged," he would say, parroting Trump. "You'll see what happens on election day."

Yea., pal, we will.

Trump's sentencing by no-BS Judge Juan Merchan on July 11 will come just four days before the Republican National Convention opens in Milwaukee, where he is expected to formally be crowned as the GOP's presidential nominee. There's little doubt, at least at this point, that Trump will win the nomination -- even if Merchan sentences him to jail, which most observers doubt will really happen.

What Crime?

But here we are with Trump the first US president to be convicted of a felony, and under present law he actually could serve as president if elected -- even if he's behind bars. That is incredible to contemplate, and if Congress had any guts, they'd change that law. However, Republicans still control the House of Representatives, so there's little chance of that.

Yes, Trump will appeal, but even if he loses and the conviction sticks, he technically could serve as president if he should defeat President Biden on November 5, which he predicted following the verdict.

"This was a rigged, disgraceful trial," Trump told reporters after leaving the courtroom. "The real verdict is going to be Nov. 5 by the people. They know what happened, and everyone knows what happened here."

That line already is being parroted by GOP sycophants like House Speaker Mike Johnson, who along with other Republican leaders showed up in court to support Trump and lambaste the proceedings on behalf of Trump, ordered not to do so by the judge who threatened to jail him if he continued such antics.

"Today is a shameful day in American history," Johnson said. "The American people rightfully see this is lawfare, and they know it is — and dangerous," he added. "President Trump will rightfully appeal this absurd verdict — and he WILL WIN."

"The weaponization of our justice system has been a hallmark of the Biden Administration, and the decision today is further evidence that Democrats will stop at nothing to silence dissent and crush their political opponents," Johnson said.

Meanwhile, people like the South Carolina MAGA pickup driver will be asked by the orange one to cough up some money for his campaign, money that could well be diverted to help pay mounting legal bills. Maybe those foolish true believers will buy some of Trump's MAGA Bibles or his pricy sneakers that he said Blacks would like because they like high-tops.

While the falsifying business records charges, of which he was found guilty, carry up to four years behind bars, it's not clear if prosecutors will seek imprisonment or if the judge would impose incarceration anyway. Most observers doubt that will happen, but it could.

Meanwhile, Trump faces three other felony indictments, although they are unlikely to be heard before the election as he's managed to pull enough strings, including the appointment of a suck-up judge in Florida, to delay those cases. He's charged with subverting American democracy by encouraging supporters to storm the Capitol on Jan. 6, 2021, to prevent Biden's election from being finalized, as well as rigging the election results in Georgia, and with mishandling classified documents at his Mar-a-Lago estate.

All of that eventually will be resolved, and those cases would carry much stiffer penalties if he were convicted.

Will the Republicans have second thoughts about anointing this loser with their nomination? While that's wishful thinking, as of now Joe Biden's opponent is an officially declared felon, a fact that should cost him some votes and enhance the president's chances of re-election.

Surely there are sensible Republicans who will refuse to vote for a convicted felon for president. Surely.

And, what about Mr. Pickup Truck man? Does he still want to know what crimes this guy committed?

◆◆◆

Trump Post-Conviction News Conference: Whining and Misdirections

By CJ Waldron

June 1, 2024

A day after he was convicted on 34 counts related to election interference and falsifying business records, Trump announced that he would hold a press conference. Media outlets touted it as an event where he would finally be asked the uncomfortable questions he's been avoiding. For hours, the media teased about what they saw as the ultimate opportunity to make him answer for his crimes.

For anyone who has been watching Trump over the past several years it will come as no surprise that, instead of the back-and-forth, question-and-answer session, it was the typical rambling and airing of grievances we've seen countless times. His typical menu of whining and misdirections. Reporters, anxious to pin him down, were left with their questions unanswered as Trump didn't take a single query. Instead, he rambled on in his usual incoherent manner, with unfinished sentences and lots of repetition, before walking away.

Circling the Wagons

Even before the jury left the courthouse, Republicans had their anger machine in overdrive. The party that once prided itself on defending law and order immediately began attacking the judge, jury, and legal system at large.

They took to the airwaves to condemn the process as nothing more than politically motivated, that the jury was biased and the judge who presided over the case was a Biden supporter whose party affiliation prevented him from rendering an unbiased ruling.

Mike Johnson

The beleaguered Speaker of the House, who fled to Mar a Lago to kiss the ring in order to stave off a threat to his leadership, called the verdict 'shameful' and urged the Supreme Court to step in and reverse the ruling upon appeal. He even attended one day of the trial, after which he echoed Trump's claim that the process was politically motivated by a corrupt justice department that had been weaponized to defeat Donald Trump.

Mitch McConnell

The outgoing Senate Minority Leader, who has been dubbed 'Moscow Mitch' for his favorable rulings towards Trump with regard to the Russia investigation, claimed the charges should have never been brought in the first place.

Elise Stefanik

Once a fierce Trump critic, Stefanik has watched her star rise as she began aligning herself with the MAGA faction. So, it should come as no surprise that she defended him. She remained in lockstep with this group following the verdict by parroting Trump's claim that he was being persecuted by a corrupt and rigged justice system.

Tim Scott

Like the others, Scott blasted the ruling and declared that it would only embolden Trump's base to propel him to victory in November. He then made the peculiar twist of claiming Trump did more for Blacks than any other president. He conveniently forgot Trump's calling BLM protestors 'thugs', or his threats of violence against them (When the looting starts, the shooting starts).

J D Vance

The congressman who has repeatedly called for investigations into journalists who have written pieces critical of Trump is now demanding the judge in the case, Juan Merchan, be investigated for violating Trump's First Amendment rights by imposing the Fab order during the trial.

Larry Hogan

The lone outlier amongst Republicans, Larry Hogan, has been threatened by the Trump campaign. His crime? While he didn't applaud the decision, he urged members of his party to respect the decision. This led Trump's senior aide Chris LaCivita to declare that Hogan's campaign for senate was effectively dead.

Whining and Misdirections

There is no small amount of hypocrisy in Republicans calling the trial politically motivated. After all, Trump's first impeachment was based on his attempt to coerce a world leader into providing damaging information on his 2020 opponent, Joe Biden.

They continue to hold endless hearings that they claim will eventually find irrefutable evidence of some form of corruption. Each time they say they have found the smoking gun that proves this, they end up with egg their faces, yet they continue to hold hearings in a vain effort to demonstrate that any appearance of impropriety is enough to declare that Biden is unfit for office.

Republicans, who claim the proceedings involving Trump are the result of the weaponization of the Department of Justice. Yet, the Congressional committee they formed to investigate this accusation only uncovered wrongdoing during the Trump administration. During his tenure, Trump had the IRS, FBI, and other government agencies investigate his perceived enemies.

The Democratic Response

Democrats have remained largely silent since the verdict was announced, keeping in line with the approach they took during the trial. Perhaps they want to be the magnanimous victors or maybe they don't want to give any fuel to the MAGA claim that the entire process is politically motivated.

At a speaking engagement on the night the verdict was announced, Trump's one-time opponent, Hillary Clinton, was able to get in a well-timed dig without mentioning Trump's name. As she opened her speech, she quipped, "Anything going on today?" which caused to audience to burst into laughter and applause.

President Biden responded to Trump's reaction to the verdict by calling him reckless and irresponsible. He further stated that it was dangerous for

Trump to call the trial rigged, indicating it could possibly result in violence. He further reiterated that no one is above the law.

The message Democrats are unified in presenting is not to gloat, but to be thankful that justice has prevailed. Perhaps as election day gets closer, they will sharpen their approach. After all, the prospect of having a convicted felon in the White House should be a bridge too far for most Americans.

There is a lot to unravel from the current political climate. Unfortunately, there won't be any answers forthcoming during any Donald Trump press conference.

◆◆◆

Guilty Verdict Has Republican Heads Exploding

By C J Waldron

June 4, 2024

Donald Trump's conviction on misuse of campaign funds has Republican heads exploding. They are calling the ruling politically motivated, blaming the Biden administration and the justice system and demanding the verdict be overturned.

But the real reason they are so angry is that they can't do anything to influence the jury's decision. Unlike the impeachment trials, they aren't able to block the verdict to allow Trump to go unpunished for his illegal actions.

Based upon his recent conviction, it's entirely possible that Trump would have lost in 2016 if the details regarding his infidelity and illegal payoff became public. Coming on the heels of the *Access Hollywood* video, it would likely be a bridge too far for many conservative voters. It could also have offset the controversy surrounding the FBI's unnecessary re-opening of the Clinton email debacle.

Trump's first impeachment trial resulted in an acquittal due to Republicans refusing to hold him accountable for his "perfect phone call" with Ukrainian President Zelensky. After the votes had been tallied, many Republicans who voted for acquittal openly admitted that while Trump had committed impeachable offenses, they rationalized their dereliction of their Constitutional duty by claiming that it was up to the voters to decide whether Trump deserved to remain in office.

Sen. Susan Collins (R-ME) went as far as to claim that Trump had learned his lesson, whatever that means. Yeah, he certainly did! He learned that no matter what he did, Republicans would always allow him to evade the consequences of his actions.

That held true in his second impeachment trial as well. Despite overwhelming evidence, Republicans remained largely united in refusing to hold him accountable for the events of January 6th. This time they used the excuse that, since Trump was no longer in office, there was nothing to back a conviction. They conveniently ignored that by holding him liable, it would prevent him from seeking office again. They further argued that if Trump was to be held accountable, if was up to the legal system to make it happen.

Now Trump's lawyers are trying to assert that the Senate acquittal meant that the charges brought by Jack Smith and the DOJ are a violation of the Double Jeopardy clause. The problem with this is that the Senate trial has no legal bearing on criminal acts. It's a political function and not a legal one, therefore Double Jeopardy does not apply.

Republican Heads Exploding

All of these machinations have led Republicans to believe that they could block any potential consequences Trump might face for his actions. Which is why they are foaming at the mouth at the recent verdict. Their powerlessness in preventing Trump from being found guilty of 34 counts of falsifying business records has their collective heads exploding.

So, the party of law and order is taking a new approach. They are slamming the judge, the jury and the legal process. MAGA followers are threatening to dox, or release the personal information including names, addresses, workplaces, family member information and any other details they consider relevant to threaten and intimidate the judge, jury and prosecuting attorneys.

Trump has gone as far as to suggest that his followers wouldn't stand for any form of punishment. He has indicated that if he were given prison time, or even put under house arrest, they would resort to violence to get his release.

They have made this claim before. Trump toady Sen. Lindsey Graham (R-SC) claimed that if Trump was indicted, his followers would take to the streets in protest, similar to the January 6th insurrection. He's been indicted four times, and there has been nary a peep other than rants on social media.

Republican lawmakers are united in their outrage. But because they cannot impact the conviction, they are doing what any mature adult would do: holding their breath, stomping their feet and demanding a do-over just as they had when they refused to accept the results of the 2020 election.

Some have even gone as far as to sign a petition declaring that they would not support any Biden initiatives or approve any of his nominations until the convictions are reversed, not that they would anyway, so this is nothing more than a hollow threat.

Others, including Speaker Mike Johnson and Trump himself, have demanded that the Supreme Court intervene to correct this perceived injustice. After all, Johnson claims to have friends on the bench and Trump, who appointed three of the current Justices, believes they will side with him out of loyalty.

The mere fact that they cannot block Trump from being punished for his crimes, like they did in both his impeachment trials, is incredibly frustrating for the MAGA base and Republicans in general. All they can do is stew and loudly protest the results.

It will do nothing to change the result, so Republican heads are literally exploding,

◆ ◆ ◆

Scared Yet? You Should Be...

By V. Susan Hutchinson

July 2, 2024

Yesterday's Supreme Court decision that gives Donald Trump immunity for his treasonous acts as President of the United States on January 6, 2021 should put the fear of God into everyone in America.

Why? Because he is not only immune for past actions as President, he is immune for the rest of his life should he regain the White House. Yes, the rest of his life.

Make no mistake, Donald Trump wants to emulate his buddy Vladimir Putin who conducts "elections" in Russia that he always wins. If Trump even allows elections to happen after 2024, he will make sure they are rigged so he can be President for life. And now as the most powerful person in the country, who SCOTUS has decided is above the law, he will target anyone he feels is against him.

Scared Yet? You Should Be

Trump's thousands, perhaps hundreds of thousands, of enemies are not just political, they are also ordinary citizens like you and me. You know, those of us who did not vote for him in 2016, 2020 and 2024 or spoke out against him on social media. He wants all of us silenced. You know his friend Elon Musk will turn over all personal information for liberals on his platform to Trump, probably without being asked.

Under a Trump regime any of us could get our door broken down and hauled off to a concentration camp -- the ones he says he will build for illegals. They will be turned into camps for his enemies as well. Just like his hero Adolf Hitler built. Presidential immunity!Media outlets?

Having options to hear left leaning or unbiased news will be a thing of the past. Only propaganda will be allowed on the airwaves. All real journalists will be put in prison so they cannot speak the truth about him anymore. Immunity for Trump if journalists want to try for legal recourse.

True Trump Supporters Will Be Safe Though, Right?

That depends on whether they stay die hard supporters once he turns America into an autocracy.

Finally figured out shredding the Constitution includes getting rid of the right to bear arms. Too late. He will come for your guns because he knows how dangerous you can be. After all he is the one who stoked the violence in you for his personal gain. And he is terrified of you turning on him with those guns if you ever wake up to the fact that he conned you.

Protesting because he took your guns? Well, if there is no First Amendment there will be no freedom of speech or right to protest, as President Trump can send the National Guard after your sorry butts to either shoot you or put you in prison. And you have no legal recourse because he has immunity.

If he sends the American terrorist groups who call themselves militias instead, he now has the power to pardon anyone who does his dirty work. This SCOTUS decision is a win for them as well.

So, I ask again: Are you scared yet? You should be.

What Can We Do?

There is still rule of law in this country; however much it is being chipped away by a Supreme Court that no longer cares about interpreting the Constitution and is only doing Trump's bidding. Only the American people have the absolute power to determine the fate of this country before it permanently slides into a mirror of Russia.

There are more Americans who stand behind our Democracy than there are Trump supporters. And we are getting angrier every day. We alone can stop Donald J. Trump by exercising OUR RIGHT TO VOTE! The modern-day equivalent of a Revolutionary War minuteman is a voter at a polling place casting a ballot to protect the Democracy our ancestors fought for in the 18th Century.

Stop Worrying About Biden. Focus on Trump

We all need to put aside any concerns over Joe Biden and realize now is not the time to waffle or bail on the Democratic Party.

We need to get young voters, minorities and everyone who is afraid for the future of their children and grandchildren to suck it up and vote against Trump's horrific plans for the America we love. There is no sitting this one out.

We can defeat this orange demon for good on November 5. If Trump tries another coup when he is defeated, he will be a private citizen and prosecuted like anyone else.

Although Trump is the main threat, we must remember that winning Congress is just as important as putting Biden back in the White House.

A Trump win with a Democratic majority in both the House and Senate means another impeachment and, this time, removal if he tries to become a dictator. Trump gets no immunity from Congress.

However, a GOP House and Senate with or without Trump as President will mean the death of America.

The Court's decision exposes Trump supporters as the fake patriots they are. A real patriot understands the founding fathers explicitly did not want anyone in the Presidency to act like a king. It is clearly spelled out in the Declaration of Independence, a declaration we are celebrating on July 4.

So, enjoy the holiday with friends and family and remember to VOTE this November so we can celebrate the American independence of 1776 and 2024.

◆◆◆

Did Biden Steal a Page from the Trump Playbook?

By C J Waldron

July 11, 2024

If there is one thing Donald Trump excels at, it is turning bad news into an opportunity. So, you have to wonder, with Biden's disastrous debate performance, did he steal a page from the Trump playbook?

Turn on the news and the lead story is certain to be the "will he or won't he" saga of whether Biden will bow out of the presidential race. And it has to be driving the media-obsessed Trump absolutely bonkers! After all, shouldn't he be dominating the headlines with his keep-em-guessing approach as to who will get the rose and become his vice president?

Isn't it just a week until his coronation in Milwaukee?

So, why isn't the media fawning over Trump, hoping to get the scoop? What's all this "Biden, Biden, Biden" coverage about? Why are they hanging on Biden's every word, hoping to catch another verbal gaffe instead of obsessing over Trump's latest insult-laden social media post?

It's like Biden is the new kid in town and people are looking at Trump with the "Oh, are you still here?" attitude. And not being the center of attention is something Trump can't stand.

No doubt Trump is harkening back to the good old days when everyone hung on his every word. You remember? When he was on trial in NY and there was gavel-to-gavel coverage for weeks on end?

Breaking News: Trump falls asleep in court!

Breaking News: Trump glances at jurors!

Breaking News: Trump passes gas in an otherwise quiet courtroom!

Trump literally held court in a daily basis as the media tracked him leaving his apartment. They fawned over him at his impromptu daily rantings behind metal barricades. Oh, where did they all go? Now it's all about Biden!

Oh well. There's always social media for attention. Except social media is being dominated by Project 2025. It's being touted as a blueprint for Trump's second term. It is also being called "Institutionalized Trumpism".

So, all things Trump without the Donald? That would mean that it wasn't about Trump at all! It was about the far right finding someone gullible enough, stupid enough and easily manipulated enough to carry out their heinous agenda.

So, instead of being an agent of change, Trump has only been a tool of the far right? Time to come up with a plan! Let's call it Agenda 47. That's better! Never mind that it is nearly identical to Project 2025. It has a shiny new name, so it must be filled with original Trump ideas.

But no. It's just Trump trying to get back into the spotlight. And his equally gullible followers will eat it up.

The old adage goes, any publicity, even bad publicity, is good. It is something Trump has been a staple for years.

Mock the disabled? Must be fake news.

Get arrested? Sell t-shirts with your mug shot on them.

Get convicted? Turn it into a fundraiser for your legal fees.

And now Joe Biden is trying to spin his horrendous debate performance into a good thing as he tries to rally the troops to support his fading attempt at re-election. Is he trying to steal a page from the Trump playbook?

Will it work? Only time will tell. Whatever the outcome, it's all the more important to Vote Blue come November.

◆◆◆

Was the Trump 'Shooting' an Inside Job?

By Bob Gatty

July 15, 2024

Many questions surrounding the July 6 Donald Trump assassination attempt in Butler, PA remain, with suspicions repeatedly expressed on social media that somehow this might have been an inside job, a ploy cooked up by Trump's team to assure 45's return to the White House.

Sort of like a scam run by his pal, Vladimir Putin.

That's hard to believe considering the tragic consequences at the event, which saw a father and husband killed by one of the would-be assassin's bullets and two other Trump supporters critically injured.

Trump Already Benefiting

Whatever the truth, there is one fact that's emerged since that shooting: Trump's chances of winning the election have vastly improved -- to 74 percent, according to the SportsHandle election odds tracker. As of this morning, the organization reported these odds:

Donald Trump - 74%

Joe Biden - 17.96%

Kamala Harris - 10.28%

"Donald Trump's lead over the field was already commanding but the unfortunate events of this weekend have raised his popularity even more. It's beginning to look evident that Joe Biden will not step down from the race, and that Donald Trump will likely have a clearer path to victory this fall than he had in either 2016 or 2020," said a spokesman for Sports Handle.

Meanwhile, new data reveals that Trump's Instagram followers have skyrocketed by over 702,000 since the shooting.

Research conducted by social media marketing experts at Viralyft.com used Social Blade and TikTok Creative Center to analyze the Trump social media follower increase and engagement, showing that his Instagram following has climbed to 26.6 million followers, or 49 percent more than Biden's 17.2 million followers.   Trump also has gained popularity on TikTok with the hashtag #Trump gaining 668 million views, #DonaldTrump gaining 282 million and #Trump2024 gaining 157 million in the past seven days worldwide.

Many questions surrounding the July 6 Donald Trump assassination attempt in Butler, PA still remain, with suspicions repeatedly expressed on social media that somehow this might have been an inside job, a ploy cooked up by Trump's team to assure 45's return to the White House.

Sort of like a scam run by his pal, Vladimir Putin.

That's hard to believe considering the tragic consequences at the event, which saw a father and husband killed by one of the would-be assassin's bullets and two other Trump supporters critically injured.

Research conducted by social media marketing experts at Viralyft.com used Social Blade and TikTok Creative Center to analyze the Trump social media follower increase and engagement, showing that his Instagram following has climbed to 26.6 million followers, or 49 percent more than Biden's 17.2 million followers.

An Inside Job?

Was this simply a tragic photo op staged by Trump, as many posters on social media suggest, to bolster his image as a fighter and claims that he's been unfairly targeted by Democrats? If so, it appears to be working -- spectacularly. And now that clenched fist image of the apparently bloodied Trump just below an American flag is being used by the Trump campaign to bolster his tough guy image at the very time that President Biden is being portrayed as frail, weak, and mentally out of it.

Here are just some of the many questions being raised on social media about the incident:

If he was actually shot in the ear -- even grazed -- by an AR 15 caliber bullet, why was there no more serious damage to his ear, face or head?

Why did the Secret Service and law enforcement not respond to eyewitness reports of the gunman on top of that factory roof only 150 yards away and take that guy down before he had a chance to shoot? He was in view of Secret Service snipers on top of other buildings nearby.

Why did the Secret Service appear to move photographers closer to the stage just before the "pop, pop, pops" were heard? Did that really happen?

If the report is true that Trump's ear was bloodied by shards of glass from the teleprompter being hit by a bullet, rather than him being grazed by a bullet, where are the photos of that teleprompter?

Why did the Secret Service personnel who surrounded Trump allow him to do his fist pump and create that now famous photo that's being plastered all over the media? It appears that in doing so, he opened himself up to being shot again if there was an accomplice out there.

Did this 20-year-old kid, a registered Republican, act alone? Did he cook this up all by himself? If so, why? He couldn't have thought that he'd get away with it.

Why did those Secret Service agents on the Trump detail not have earpieces for communication? Photos from the scene appear to show that they did not. If that was the case, how could they know there was not another shooter ready to finish the job?

Why were his shoes off? And if he had just been shot, why did he care about his shoes?

How was it possible that just an hour after the incident T-shirts with that image were for sale on the Internet?

The Truth will Out

Whatever the truth, it will emerge -- it always does. There will be multiple investigations, no doubt Congressional hearings, and hopefully we will know the truth. But the question is when and how? Already, the incident -- staged or not -- is playing in favor of Trump at absolutely the worst time for Biden, whose candidacy is threatened because of continued questions about his health and mental capacity.

What was the first thing Biden's campaign announced? That their anti-Trump ads would be pulled as soon as possible. It was a decent response, one out of respect for the former president. But what did the Republicans do? Sen. J. D. Vance (R-OH), before Trump picked him as his vice presidential nominee, wrote on X:

"The central premise of the Biden campaign is that President Donald Trump is an authoritarian fascist who must be stopped at all costs," Sen. J.D. Vance (R-Ohio). "That rhetoric led directly to President Trump's attempted assassination."

Declared Rep. Ronnie Jackson (R-TX), "Trump-deranged Left-wing LU-NATICS that parade around MSNBC and other FAKE NEWS "outlets" demonizing Trump and calling him Hitler are DIRECTLY RESPONSIBLE for this violent attack on President Trump's life!! They have BLOOD on their hands. ENOUGH of the VIOLENT RHETORIC! AMERICA IS PISSED!!!!"

Yes, Mr. Congressman, America is pissed. We're sick and tired of Trump's hate-filled rhetoric and that of irresponsible politicians like you. We're sick and tired of our fellow citizens being suckered by the serial charlatan, Donald J. Trump.

Former GOP Rep. Adam Kinzinger wrote on X following the incident, "The Trump campaign and surrogates will try to intimidate Biden supporters from going after the former President politically. Do not let up. Trump is a threat to democracy, and he must be stopped. Every rational person knows that means politically. DO NOT let them twist your words and intimidate you. Trump must be beaten at the ballot box."

Listen to him.

◆◆◆

What is Trump's Spaghetti Strategy?

By C J Waldron

September 9, 2024

When it comes to his reelection strategy, the Trump campaign seems satisfied with throwing out baseless accusations and name-calling instead of offering a coherent view of what they will do if given a second chance to ruin the country. It's an approach many people take when making pasta. They throw it at the wall and see if it sticks.

It's Trump's spaghetti strategy.

He has called Kamala an "ultra-liberal", whatever that is. He has tried recycling old derogatory labels such as Lyin' Kamala and Crooked Kamala. He has repeatedly mispronounced her name (or perhaps he is just too old to remember how to pronounce it properly?). He even tried out an odd spelling of her name (Kamabla) hoping that would catch on.

None of it has stuck with his MAGA faithful. The idea that one of these childish taunts would have the crowd chanting the way they shouted, "Lock her up!" during the 2016 campaign has yet to catch on leaving Trump prone to even more rants such as mocking her laugh and how she often smiles. Can anyone remember ever hearing Trump laugh?

This would be fine if he was just your average senior citizen shouting at the neighborhood teens to stay off his lawn. But this is a person who is vying for the job of the most powerful person in the free world. His unhinged rants and immature outbursts have world leaders on edge as Trump praises autocrats while he threatens democracies.

He Said What?

Donald Trump's speeches will never go down in history. There is no "Ask not what your country will do for you…" or "The only thing you have to fear is…". There isn't even a "Read my lips". Brilliant oratory is not his strength, yet his base clings to every word as if they were hearing from the Almighty himself.

Trump's speeches are the Tale of Two Trumps. There is teleprompter Trump where he spouts the same false claims of a rigged system and a stolen election. Add to this his new boast of overturning *Roe v Wade.* Toss in a few conspiracy theories and you pretty much have the same well-rehearsed script that you hear at any one of his rallies.

But when Trump goes off script, oh boy! There are wild claims about windmills, ramblings about sharks and electric motors and odd sound effects allegedly mimicking gunfire or missile launchings.

And let's not forget how this "stable genius" has repeatedly thanked the late, great Hannibal Lecter for having a friend for dinner while he brags about "Acing" a cognitive test that is actually meant to detect dementia.

It is then Trump is likely to try out one of his latest taunts, but unlike many of his earlier rallies, these childish jibes haven't yielded to raucous chants that were the centerpieces of his previous campaigns.

Perhaps Donald is losing his edge? Or perhaps the truly faithful are losing interest. Like a once-popular song, Trump's routine seems to be fading, making room for a new, younger, more energetic face.

Next?

When most candidates for president choose someone to be their second-in-command, the typical goal is to select someone who will balance the ticket, bringing in voters who would otherwise want someone else. JFK, from New England, famously opted for Lyndon Johnson, from Texas, to offset what many viewed as Kennedy's greatest weakness, his youth, with the seasoned Johnson. Political pundits have credited this choice as the reason Kennedy was able to eke out a narrow victory over then-Vice President Richard Nixon.

Trump's advisors urged him to make a similar decision by choosing someone from a swing state to stabilize the ticket should Trump go off on one of his rants. But Trump being Trump ignored their advice and opted for loyalty over political common sense. With his seemingly insurmountable lead over Joe Biden, Trump decided that his choice for a running mate would have no impact on the outcome of the election.

Despite JD Vance calling Trump an American Hitler, Vance was selected among several, more suitable options. It seems he had undergone a conversion and was now full-on MAGA. And Republicans were quick to hail

Vance as the future of the MAGA movement, until…

It didn't take long until Vance's past statements came back to haunt him. It was revealed that he called women who didn't have children "childless cat ladies" who were miserable and wanted to spread their misery to others. He later claimed that post-menopausal women were obligated to assist in the raising of their grandchildren. Not very good advice when you are trying to court the women's vote.

Republicans were outraged when Hillary Clinton referred to them as a basket of deplorables, but apparently childless cat ladies is okay in their book.

Once Joe Biden stepped aside, Trump turned his sights on Kamala Harris. During a conference of Black journalists, Trump accused her of using her race to garner votes and that she had only recently "turned Black". He completely ignored the fact that Harris attended Howard University, a Historically Black College, that she was a member of several Black organizations.

Being his running mate, Vance felt obligated to defend Trump's comment. First, he declared that Harris was being disingenuous because she claimed to be the first Indian American elected to Congress. To Vance and Trump, this proved she wasn't really identifying as Black. Never mind that most of us have multiple lineages due to our parents' backgrounds. Trump himself has a German father and a Scottish mother, but he only wants to recognize his Whiteness.

Vance went on to claim that Harris was a chameleon who changed her identity to suit whatever crowd she was facing. Yet Vance has gone under multiple names during his lifetime, so who is really the chameleon here?

But it seems only Trump can be Trump. When Vance went after Harris's running mate, Tim Walz, over discrepancies in his military record, the public, in particular veterans, were not having it. They blasted Vance over his comments and demanded he apologize for denigrating someone with 24 years of military service. Yet, when Trump used the sacred grounds of Arlington Cemetery for a campaign photo op, there was some outrage, but little protest from the MAGA faithful.

Comrade, Communist, Marxist, and an oldie but a goodie, the radical Left, have all been attempts by Trump to label Kamala Harris. None of them has stuck and the race is currently neck and neck as Election Day fast approaches.

But when Tim Walz referred to JD Vance as "weird", that stuck.

◆◆◆

Chapter Three

Understanding Project 2025

This chapter examines the Heritage Foundation's effort to transform the government through a process called Project 2025. Lean to the Left writers CJ Waldron and V. Susan Hutchinson explore how allies of Donald Trump hope to increase the power of the presidency, eliminate career government positions, and cede regulatory responsibility to the individual states. It is critical for voters to understand key parts of this manifesto, in context with current and future GOP proposals. The statements in Project 2025 are, at best, misleading with outright lies, twisted interpretations of the Constitution, and personal opinions sprinkled throughout, and much of the document has been incorporated into the GOP Platform. So, beware.

Project 2025: Dismantling Democracy

By C J Waldron

July 9, 2024

If Donald Trump is re-elected in November, the cornerstone if his second administration will be Project 2025. It is a program authored by members of the once Conservative think tank, now full-blown MAGA, Heritage Foundation. It's subtitled *The Presidential Transition Project*.

So, what is Project 2025?

According to Heritage Foundation President Kevin Roberts, it is "…the second American Revolution which will remain bloodless if the left allows it to be."

This ominous comment shouldn't be ignored. The Heritage Foundation is not a group to make idle threats. After all, they vowed to undo *Roe v Wade*. So, it should come as no surprise that they are the ones who recommended the three justices Donald Trump was allowed to appoint.

Despite it being touted as a blueprint for Trump's second term, he has alternately claimed to have no knowledge of the plan while also saying he disagrees with parts of it. As details of the plan become public, Trump is now trying to distance himself from the Heritage Foundation by disavowing the plan.

His reasons are obvious. Trump is never one to want to share the limelight, so should he win, he wants credit for coming up with the vile plan all on his own. The goal of which is to institutionalize Trumpism beyond his time in office.

Former RNC Chair Michael Steele ridiculed Trump's dual stance. He also mocked his denial of knowing anyone associated with the project since some were high-ranking officials in his administration.

The project is built on four pillars:

Pillar I—this volume—puts in one place a consensus view of how major federal agencies must be governed and where disagreement exists brackets out these differences for the next President to choose a path.

Pillar II is a personnel database that allows candidates to build their own professional profiles and coalition members to review and voice their recommendations. These recommendations will then be collated and shared with the President-elect's team, greatly streamlining the appointment process.

Pillar III is the Presidential Administration Academy, an online educational system taught by experts from the coalition. For the newcomer, this will explain how the government functions and how to function in government. For the experienced, they will host in-person seminars with advanced training and set the bar for what is expected of senior leadership.

In Pillar IV—the Playbook—They are forming agency teams and drafting transition plans to move out upon the President's utterance of "so help me God."

(From the Playbook *Mandate for Leadership*)

Some of Project 2025's priorities include:

Slashing employment in the federal government and muzzling "woke propaganda at every level of government"

Eliminating the Department of Education and its "woke-dominated system of public schools"

Prohibiting the FBI from fighting misinformation and disinformation

Ending the "war on fossil fuels" and allowing further development on Native American lands

Ending active FBI investigations that are "contrary to the national interest"

Reducing benefits to veterans and active-duty troops while rewarding private contractors

When the Founding Fathers established our federal government, it did so with the understanding that there would be three branches: The Executive, the Legislative and the Judiciary. Each branch would be equal, with a system of checks and balances meant to ensure that no one branch was more powerful than the other. The legislative branch made the laws, the executive branch carried out the laws and the judicial branch interpreted the laws.

It was all working fine, with a few bumps that needed to be ironed out, but over almost 250 years, the process worked. Even a Civil War did not disrupt the country's ability to maintain a functioning government.

Project 2025 wants to obliterate that process through something called the Unitary Executive Theory. This would elevate the office of the president to have the authority to overrule Congress and the courts, making the president a De facto monarch, answerable to no one.

And it's already happening

The recent Supreme Court decision giving Trump immunity for "official acts" means he could go unpunished for the events of January 6th, his efforts to overturn the 2020 election results and even his possession of classified documents. Should he regain the White House, there's no telling how far an unrestrained Donald Trump would go.

Trump has vowed to get rid of the Department of Education. Project 2025 is proposing similar actions to eliminate the "woke agenda" in public schools. Some states aren't waiting for it to happen. Florida has already enacted the "Don't Say Gay" law that prohibits even the discussion of alternative lifestyles in the classroom, including forcing teachers to address students by the gender on their birth certificate even if they identify otherwise. Public schools in Louisiana and Oklahoma have enacted polices to push a right-wing biased Christian agenda. Classrooms in Louisiana are being forced to display a copy of the Ten Commandments while the Oklahoma State Superintendent is requiring a Bible be present in every classroom and Bible lessons be part of every curriculum.

Project 2025 represents a serious threat to democracy. It will usher in an era of one-party rule with no accountability for those in power. By eliminating government positions that do not align with the MAGA agenda, it promises to undo the system the Founding Fathers intended.

◆◆◆

Understanding Project 2025: Abortion

By V. Susan Hutchinson

July 20, 2024

Abortion is just one of the hot button topics for voters in Project 2025. This article is intended to educate voters on the potential future of abortion in America. We'll discuss the context of the word abortion as used in Project 2025, provide data that challenges their proposals, and put "banning abortion" in a broader context that also discusses the potential consequences of their actions.

Voters should not rely on bullet points about Project 2025 posted on social media sites to educate themselves. Those quick lists are intended to stir up emotions, not explain what is in the document or how the "Christian" minority wants to shove their culture down everyone's throats.

As you will see below, these bulleted lists only point to a planning document to lay blame. They are also fodder for Trump and MAGA politicians to say, "that's not what we are saying," thus making it appear that they are not the extremists they are, and possibly sway some undecided voters.

Project 2025 does not specifically call for a national abortion ban nor use the words "restrict access to abortion and contraception." So why are there so many claiming the document calls for a federal ban on abortion and how are these terms presented in the document?

The word "abortion" is mentioned 12 times in Project 2025, none next to the word "ban". In the forward alone, it is there three times. The last paragraph using the term abortion puts it in context of "pro-life and pro-family policies" and discusses the need to use federal power for "robust protections for the unborn" with bans on federal *funding* for abortion. The only "solution" proposed is to explore alternative options, especially adoption, which should receive federal and state support. The type of that support is not stated but assumed to be financial.

94

Congressional Bill H.R. 431 – Life at Conception Act

This bill was introduced in the House January 20, 2023, and is currently pending in the Judiciary Committee. Its stated goal is "To implement equal protection for the right to life of each born and preborn human person, and pursuant to the duty and authority of the Congress, including Congress' power under Article I, Section 8 to make necessary and proper laws, and Congress' power under Section 5 of the 14th article of amendment to the Constitution of the United States, the Congress hereby declares that the right to life guaranteed by the Constitution is vested in each human being. However, nothing in this Act shall be construed to authorize the prosecution of any woman for the death of her unborn child."

The bill defines a human person/being to include "each and every member of the species homo sapiens at all stages of life, including the moment of fertilization, cloning, or other moment at which an individual member of the human species comes into being."

This bill does not call for a national abortion ban. Rather, it tries to define morally, not scientifically, when an assemblance of living tissue can be called a human being. It uses an amendment created to define American citizenship for former slaves to justify any legislative actions taken to protect these newly defined "humans."

This is just one glaring example of twisting the Constitution to support an ultra-conservative agenda and imply our founding document and its amendments support their new vision for the country.

Two parts of the 14th Amendment are important to know and put into context for this new definition of life.

It states, "No State shall make or enforce any laws which shall abridge the privileges or immunities of citizens of the United States; nor shall any State deprive any person of life, liberty, or property, without due process of law; nor deny to any person within its jurisdiction the equal of the laws." It concludes by saying "The Congress shall have the power to enforce, by appropriate legislation, the provisions of this article."

In short, states can pass legislation about citizenship, but at the federal level, Congress has the power to question the legality of their actions, decide if it fits the description of a citizen per the 14th Amendment and take appropriate actions to overturn state laws related to citizenship.

Once fertilized embryos are declared humans conceived in the United States, they become citizens if H.R. 431 becomes law. Citizenship then comes within the boundaries of the 14th Amendment. An ultra-conservative "Christian" based Congress could then decide that legal abortion implemented at the state level is unconstitutional and force it to be overturned. States rights are important to the GOP, but only for states that fully support its agenda.

Essentially, this bill would become a jumping off point for a more specifically defined national ban on abortion without specifically stating that is the intended purpose.

Adoption is the Solution?

According to the Guttmacher Institute, the *Dobbs* decision to overturn *Roe v. Wade* resulted in a total of 1,037,000 abortions in 2023 in states without total bans, which is an 11 percent increase in abortions since 2020. The data does not include self-managed (i.e. using medication) abortions and the institute suggests these have increased as well.

The most recent information on adoption and foster care comes from an internet search and shows 2021 data published by the U.S. Department of Health and Human Services. The number of children in foster care is rising with over 391,000 in foster homes. A little less than one third are eligible for adoption and wait three or more years to be adopted. Of those adopted, 29 percent were under nine with an average age of six. Financially, 93 percent of parents who adopted needed subsidies or post adoption services, which are costly.

Of the children in foster care, 9 percent aged out of the system with no financial support, 25 percent did not have a high school diploma or GED, putting into question their employment possibilities and increasing the possibility they would enter the criminal justice system.

What happens once abortion is banned in every state?

Actions Have Consequences

As you can see, connecting the proposal from Project 2025 calling for protecting the unborn along with Congress's plan to redefine humans while creating a convoluted way to enact a disguised national abortion ban using a Constitutional Amendment gives voters a clearer understanding of what is at stake. The combined strategy gives Trump, and others who claim to not support a national ban, cover for traditional Republicans or independent voters who want abortion only decided at the state level.

If H.R. 431 becomes law, it will not just affect abortion rights; it will bring contraception that impedes the implantation of a "person" into it as well as changing the rules about IVF. The next logical step from this would be to ban contraception that prevents an ovum from dropping out of the ovaries, most likely by creating legislation that now calls them "potential" human beings that need protection.

As far as the proposed Project 2025 solution to all those hundreds of thousands of babies who will now be born, there is no plan on how adoption and foster care systems will handle the increase or where all these adoptive parents will come from, but maybe that is by design. The "Christian" right in America is all about doing what they want with no care for those who are affected by their actions or the impact to American society.

Does this mean when the time comes for addressing the consequences of banning abortion nationwide there will be forced adoption? Or is the plan to merely let these children languish in a system where many will remain until they age out before going into to a new society that cares more about them before birth and turns a blind eye when they struggle to survive?

◆◆◆

Understanding Project 2025: Save the Children

By C J Waldron

July 23, 2024

The foreword to the Project 2025 was written by the president of the Heritage Foundation, Dr. Kevin Roberts. Yes, the very same Kevin Roberts who threatened a bloody coup if the Left didn't simply roll over and accept what he called the Second American Revolution.

He begins by crediting the modern Conservative movement to Ronald Reagan 44 years ago, although many political scholars would attribute the modern movement to Barry Goldwater in 1964. However, it would be easier to accept the view of a winning candidate than one who was soundly trounced, and Nixon was definitely not an option, so he settled on Reagan.

After bashing Jimmy Carter, Roberts goes on the paint a version of Reagan's America in the vein of his "shining city on a hill" reference, only to have his vision destroyed in the 1990s by the Radical Left during the Clinton era.

He spews the typical Christian Nationalist propaganda that pictures America as a morally bankrupt, crime-ridden, drug addicted nation that has lost its way and only they have the solution to fix whatever ills currently afflict our trouble nation. He claims that America can only be saved by adopting these four guiding principles that he calls *the Conservative Promise:*

Restore the family as the centerpiece of American life and protect our children.

Dismantle the administrative state and return self-governance to the American people.

Defend our nation's sovereignty, borders, and bounty against global threats.

Secure our God-given individual rights to live freely—what our Constitution calls "the Blessings of Liberty."

He devotes the rest of the foreword to detailing how the next Conservative president, Donald Trump, is to go about turning these principles into reality. It is a blueprint of the White Christian Nationalist agenda they have been spouting for years, yet this is the best opportunity they have had to creating the very nation they have been envisioning.

PROMISE #1: RESTORE THE FAMILY AS THE CENTERPIECE OF AMERICAN LIFE AND PROTECT OUR CHILDREN.

A consistent mantra of MAGA is the depiction of Democrats as a Satan-loving cabal of pedophiles. It's a rehash of the anti-Semitic trope, Blood Libel that prevailed in Europe.

Because they do not study history, many MAGAs believe this to be something unique to Democrats. It was re-introduced into the American political landscape during the 2016 Presidential Election as Pizzagate, and has since been used to attack teachers who they allege are "grooming" students by presenting lessons aimed at sexualizing them, making them easy prey for pedophiles.

Of course, they have no evidence to support this outlandish accusation, but that hasn't prevented numerous Republican-led legislatures from introducing measures designed to address this non-issue.

Roberts echoes the Christian Nationalist view of marriage as being between a man and a woman, rejecting any acceptance of same-sex marriages as being *unnatural*. He blames the acceptance of same-sex marriages as the reason for the moral decay of our American culture.

He further states that unwed mothers are another reason for the decline in our moral values. Roberts goes on to imply that 70 percent of all Black children are fatherless by lumping absentee dads with those who simply aren't married. He claims this is the primary reason behind increased poverty rates, crime and drug abuse while trying to connect these ills to the Black population alone.

Roberts views the lack of participation in the church as progressive wokeism. He asserts that the Left is trying to reject churches' tax-exempt status as a prime example of this. He ignores that the reason some churches have had their status questioned is their morphing into a political body rather than a religious one.

In a truly head-spinning twist of logic, Roberts demands that terms related to gender equity, race, sexual orientation and reproductive rights be removed from every federal document. The truly insane part of this demand is that he claims it is protecting our First Amendment rights!

So, taking away our freedom of speech is somehow protecting it?

The right has a disturbing obsession with pornography. They want people to believe that it is the central theme of "Woke" indoctrination of our children. As a result, they want to allow more parental control over what is being taught in the classroom, making banning books a central tenet of their approach to their child's education as they seek to save the children. *(Author's Note: As an educator with almost 40 years' experience in the classroom, I can attest to the fact that there are two types of parents:*

1. Parents who are unconcerned with their child's education. They do not attend school events or take part in teacher conferences. They will not address their child's academic or behavioral issues and avoid contact with their child's teachers

2. The "helicopter parent" who is overly involved with their child's academic life. If their child isn't getting the grades the parent expects, they will invariably blame the teacher and demand immediate changes.)

Another claim by the Right is that students are being indoctrinated to hate America as teachers saturate their curriculum with Critical Race Theory. While they are unable to define what it means, they have vowed to eliminate it from America's classrooms. This is an easy fix since it has never been a part of any educational process, so the Right can claim victory for expunging something that was never there in the first place.

If nothing else, the Right is expert at assigning blame. Instead of taking responsibility for enabling their child by providing them with expensive electronics, they blame social media for its corruptive impact on their child's life. They claim that the addictive qualities of these platforms are responsible for the marked increase in mental illness in children. All the while these same parents use these electronic babysitters to avoid interacting with their own children.

Roberts concludes that the breakdown of the American family can be directly attributed to a woman's right to choose. He champions the *Dobbs* decision as something that will return America to the core family values it asserts the *Conservative Promise* is aimed at attaining.

◆◆◆

Understanding Project 2025: The Department of Education

By V. Susan Hutchinson

July 25, 2024

One thing you can say about Project 2025 and everyone who was involved in its creation is that they are angry about the ever-growing diversity of race, gender, and religion in America, all of which drives the abominable

101

"woke" agenda that is so detrimental to American children.

Their plan to re-instate Caucasian dominance is multi-pronged and grooming the next generations through the American education system is one way to ensure that dominance remains intact for future generations.

The expectation for parents when it comes to the education of their children should be that it gives them a broad base of knowledge, so as adults they will be able function better in society, make more intelligent choices in their lives and, possibly, further their education after high school to get better paying jobs.

Project 2025 prefers to focus not on improving curriculums and supplying better tools to teachers but weeding out perceived cultural and religious issues in our school system all while having the federal government pay for it.

Although Project 2025 contains graphs showing trends in test scores for various subjects, they are curiously placed in sections with no real references to them. There is no discussion on projected trends or what overall improvement in education will look like under their plan.

The gameplan appears to be show random "look at how bad things are" data and imply that taking a wrecking ball to the department to eliminate the rampant "woke" agenda in our school systems will magically make those scores rise.

This article addresses just some of the plans for the Department of Education under a new conservative regime.

The Department of Education

The Project 2025 overall mission for the Department of Education seems to be parental self-interest. The opening statement for education states "Federal education policy should be limited and, ultimately, the federal

Department of Education should be eliminated."

The call is for empowerment to be placed at the student and family level and give them the right to decide what is best for everyone, not just their own child. To support their argument, Project 2025 references economist Milton Freeman who said education should be publicly funded, but government should not be allowed to make decisions about education.

This is a very bad idea.

The Department of Education, like other federal agencies, provides needed guidelines to standardize academic programs and protect the interests of every student. Ultra-conservative parents, who fight culture wars daily, would now have the power to impose their bias and hatred on every child to keep them ignorant, as well. Placing the responsibility in the hands of parents could potentially lead to oppression of minorities in some communities, which prevents them from realizing their full potential later in life.

Dismantling the Department of Education

The Department of Education has been restructured many times between its inception in 1867 and the creation of its current state in 1979. Their mission is "... to promote student achievement and preparation for global competitiveness by fostering education excellence and ensuring equal access."

To achieve these goals the department establishes policies for federal financial aid, which includes the distribution and monitoring of funds and prohibits discrimination to ensure equal access to education. Basically, the Department of Education wants students, regardless of race, religion, or gender identity to be educated on a level playing field while making sure adequate funding is available and properly used by all schools to serve the needs of students.

The Project 2025 plan calls for cutting programs within the department or moving them to other federal departments, such as Labor, Health and

Human Services and the Department of Justice. They also propose changes to how state schools are funded or the elimination of some offices completely.

Some of these programs provide regulations for funding poor areas and protection from discrimination of minorities. The ensuing chaos from the implementation of Project 2025 will put the future of millions of children in jeopardy.

The Office of Elementary and Secondary Education (OESE) is just one of the targets in Project 2025. It calls for cutting programs or re-allocating them to other federal agencies. One key point is to "Transfer Title I, Part A, which provides federal funding for lower income school districts, to the Department of Health and Human Services, specifically the Administration for Children and Families. It should be administered as a no-strings-attached formula block grant."

Moving school funding to a department that is not designed to handle the uniqueness of educational needs is detrimental to our school systems, especially those in low-income areas. Block grants have far less oversight than the current federal funding system and can lead to abuse and corruption in local school boards.

The use of block grants is a favored term throughout the education section as well as other departments.

Funding Education

Project 2025 calls for "Advancing Education Freedom." This means parents should be given options to "improve outcomes." This is a self-serving approach to education that allows "improvements" for only select students, not all, helps suppress American minorities and leads to the widening of the wealth gap in America.

Educational freedom is for those who have the desire, but not necessarily the money. Project 2025 has the perfect solution to allow parents to choose the "best" schools for their children. The federal government will deposit taxpayer money into Education Savings Accounts (ESA) so parents can exercise this newfound freedom. Parents who can easily cover the cost of sending their children to private school would now be able to use taxpayer money instead for any private school, including those that are not state accredited.

And parents who want more of a religious indoctrination instead of the teaching of useful skills will be able to use federal money, too.

Bigoted parents also benefit from the ESA. Don't like your child going to school with minorities? Or they shouldn't learn slavery was a brutal practice or be exposed to children of same sex couples? Here is some money so you can shelter them from the realities of the world.

Education Freedom: The New School Segregation

When it comes to postsecondary education costs, which are prohibitive for millions of students, Project 2025 states "Taxpayers should expect their investments in higher education to generate economic productivity. When the federal government lends money to individuals for a postsecondary education, taxpayers should expect those borrowers to repay."

It's hard to generate economic productivity when the exorbitant interest on student debt makes it, in some cases, virtually impossible to pay off before retirement or puts the burden on parents and grandparents who should be looking out for their own financial security in retirement. This is just another example of expanding the wealth gap.

Even if minority students get a quality education in a poor community and have the test scores to enter college, Project 2025 wants you to know getting a student loan to pay for it means you lose your right to the pursuit of happiness when you graduate. You can't be happy and in deep debt.

Making Gender Identity Disappear

Project 2025 makes it clear there is no place in America for anyone who identifies as LGBTQ+, especially in our schools. Conservatives cannot grasp the concept that in today's world the sex of a child can no longer be based solely on physical attributes, and they must be wiped from existence.

If only on paper.

The forward to the Project 2025 plan states, "The noxious tenets of "critical race theory" and "gender ideology" should be excised from curricula in every public school in the country. These theories poison our children..." The hatred of those they want to marginalize in society is further expressed as the claim that sex reassignment of a minor child is child abuse that has to end.

Project 2025 takes issue particularly with Title IX from the Office of Civil Rights. The claim is "...there is no scientific or legal basis for redefining "sex" to "sexual orientation and gender identity" in this law. Conservatives want all these references stripped from this law.

Conclusions

Thomas Jefferson was a strong proponent of education stating "Educate and inform the whole mass of the people... They are the only sure reliance for the preservation of our liberty."

Project 2025 does not provide a plan for America that Jefferson or any of our founding fathers would approve. Their plan shreds the idea that every American has the right to life, liberty and the pursuit of happiness. Their plans to tear down our public education system will result in a continued cycle of poverty for every in poor communities, not just minorities.

The goal of the Heritage Foundation, Donald Trump and his all-in Republican party is for ignorance to run rampant across America as the uneducated do not have the skills to realize they are their victims too.

◆ ◆ ◆

Understanding Project 2025: A White Christian Nation

By C J Waldron

July 29, 2024

PROMISE #2: DISMANTLE THE ADMINISTRATIVE STATE AND RETURN SELF-GOVERNANCE TO THE AMERICAN PEOPLE.

The mythical Deep State is the boogeyman of the Right. As a result, they fault this shadowy bureaucratic apparatus for limiting the ability of Donald Trump to enact many of his MAGA policies during his first term. Their solution is to create a government that is filled with MAGA loyalists and create an Executive branch that has no Congressional oversight, known as the Unitary Executive Theory.

The foreword to the Project 2025 was written by the president of the Heritage Foundation, Dr. Kevin Roberts. He proposes that we "put the federal government back to work for the American people" by reducing the size of the federal bureaucracy and eliminating career federal workers to be replaced by those who adhere to the principles of the *Conservative Promise.* He claims that a smaller government would be more effective and efficient while allowing the goals of the Right to be more easily enacted.

In an attack on Diversity, Equity and Inclusion (DEI), Roberts states "Woke bureaucrats at the Pentagon" could no longer "force troops to attend "training" seminars about "white privilege". With the Supreme Court rolling back the impacts of Affirmative Action, *Project 2025* is proposing to further segregate the government, particularly the military, by stripping away many of the protections in the name of restoring the military into the hands of "highly skilled servicemen and women who can protect the homeland and our interests overseas".

His implication is that America is weaker with a more diverse military, and therefore more vulnerable. The net effect would be to have a military that was more aligned to the White Christian Nationalist agenda which would also be more loyal to the *Conservative Promise*.

Like Donald Trump's *Agenda 47, Project 2025* wants to eliminate the Department of Education. Roberts states "Bureaucrats at the Department of Education inject racist, anti-American, ahistorical propaganda into America's classrooms". Therefore, by eliminating this department, it would free the states to adopt a more Conservative Christian Nationalist curriculum.

Louisiana and Oklahoma have already begun this process. Louisiana has ordered that every classroom must post a copy of the Ten Commandments while the State School Superintendent of Oklahoma is mandating that every classroom have a Bible and include the Bible in their curriculum.

Another proposal is to reign in the pesky Environmental Protection Agency whose annoying rules and regulations have stifled the growth of Big Business by instituting choking restrictions on their ability to increase production. Since many of these rules are the result of what the Right calls the "Climate Change Hoax", this department would be curtailed, or even eliminated under the new Conservative administration.

Like abortion and Affirmative Action, the ultra-Conservative majority of the Supreme Court has already set this into motion by limiting the power of the EPA and making the courts the arbiters of any rules a business seeks to oppose, overturning the Chevron decision.

Despite the fact we learned in elementary school that there are three equal branches of the federal government, *Project 2025* claims that the true intent of the Founding Fathers was to create a hierarchical system, with the Executive branch having the lion's share of power. It is what is known as the Unitary Executive Theory.

This form of government removes any form of Congressional oversight of the president. So, the president would no longer be subject to impeachment for any alleged illegal actions. This has been further bolstered by the recent Supreme Court decision that declared that the president enjoys immunity from prosecution when such actions are in the performance of "official acts" of the president.

Project 2025 claims that a more powerful Executive branch would be able to reign in government spending and put Federal tax dollars to better use by funneling them to areas that are more supportive of the *Conservative Promise*, such as securing the Southern Border, while cutting funding for foreign aid and reckless spending on groups like NATO. All of it is part of the Republicans' effort to create a White Christian nation, to the detriment of anyone who does not fit that description.

◆◆◆

Understanding Project 2025: America First

By C J Waldron

July 31, 2024

PROMISE #3: DEFEND OUR NATION'S SOVEREIGNTY, BORDERS, AND BOUNTY AGAINST GLOBAL THREATS.

Ever since Donald Trump descended the escalator to announce his candidacy for the 2016 presidential election, it has been a constant message that most of our society's ills are the result of immigrants flooding our nation, resulting in ever increasing crimes, a drug abuse epidemic and stealing jobs from hard working Americans.

He has led rallies with the chant "Build the Wall" as his solution to what has been depicted as the crisis on the Southern Border and has accused Democrats of advocating for open borders.

These distortions of facts (and outright lies) are presented in *Project 2025*, which claims the flood of illegal immigrants coming over the Southern

Border is suppressing wages and leading to the increase in violent crime despite statistics showing that wages are rising, and violent crime is down.

Heritage Foundation President Dr. Kevin Roberts claims Democrats have "more in common with a socialist" and more and more illegal immigration are, as Donald Trump put it, "poisoning the blood of our country", a comment that has been compared to the words of Adolf Hitler. Those on the Right assert that this flood of illegal immigrants is part of what they call "The Great Replacement Theory", whereupon those who illegally enter the country will overwhelm the ballot boxes by voting against those who support the Conservative agenda.

Roberts demonstrates his lack of history by declaring that Democrats support the open borders policies of German theologian Dietrich Bonhoeffer. He ignores the fact the Bonhoeffer was executed for his part in Valkyrie, which was a plot to assassinate Adolf Hitler. Instead, he wants those on the Right to blindly associate anyone German with being a Nazi.

Roberts further distorts the facts by saying that the rise in violent crime is diverting needed funding from struggling public schools. This contradicts the policies of the Right that promote school choice, which truly strips public school budgets to support unregulated charter schools. Although they will deny it, this is a blatant effort to re-institute school segregation by making it easier for the wealthy to send their children to private schools while public education struggles to obtain the basic necessities.

Slashing Spending

Republicans have always claimed to be the party of fiscal responsibility, so it should come as no surprise that *Project 2025* aims at slashing federal spending. They would do so by dismantling or reallocating multiple federal agencies, leading to the dismissal of up to a million federal workers, The Departments of Education, Homeland Security, the Transportation Security Administration(TSA), the Environmental Protection Agency(EPA), and the Department of Housing and Urban Development(HUD) would all be eliminated.

The Federal Emergency Management Agency (FEMA) would also be eliminated with its tasks of disaster preparedness and response being divided among the Department of the Interior or the Department of Transportation with the remaining tasks allocated to the Cybersecurity and Infrastructure Agency. However, the costs of both preparedness and clean up would be shifted to the states.

The Department of Veteran's Affairs would be highly restructured with many services privatized and actual contact personnel would be replaced by automated chat bots. Veterans would lose the ability to be treated by those familiar with the unique health issues they face and instead would be forced to rely upon local medical facilities that are already overburdened.

The Centers for Disease Control and Prevention (CDC), once the main source of information during the COVID pandemic, would be divided into two agencies: one gathering scientific data and one making public health recommendations and policies. Testing and public health guidance would be shifted to the private sector where competing companies could offer varying interpretations of major health issues.

Most concerning, the Department of Justice, once the independent arm of government that held the Executive Branch accountable, would be placed under the control of the president, allowing him to use these personnel as his own personal "Gestapo police" to unfairly target anyone he perceives as his enemy.

By claiming to reign in Big Government, *Project 2025* is only making it easier for those in power to maintain their grip while denying a majority of Americans the right to have the very services their tax dollars are intended to support.

Does this sound like America First to you?

◆◆◆

Understanding Project 2025: Healthcare

By V. Susan Hutchinson

August 4, 2024

The American healthcare system is and has, for a long time, been a for profit business. The average annual salary across the country is $59,428 and Americans pay on average $13,493 per person per year for their healthcare, which is twice what other wealthy countries spend.

With the rising cost for housing, gas, food, and utilities a lot of American families need two incomes to cover basic living expenses. Heaven help those with a chronic illness, children with cancer or are also caretakers for elderly parents.

On the other side of the coin are the insurance companies who care nothing for families, especially those who already find it hard to pay premiums, co-pays, and exorbitant prescription costs. Fourth quarter earnings for 2023 show United Healthcare raking in $22.4 billion in profits, up 11.2 percent over 2022. Even though Humana was down 11.3 percent from 2022 they still managed to make $2.5 billion.

Project 2025 lays out a plan for healthcare companies to make even bigger profits every year. All while saying they want patients to be their focus.

Five Goals for Reforming the Department of Health and Human Services

In the introduction to the section on the Department of Health and Human Services (HHS), author Roger Severino makes a very true statement that "HHS activities personally impact the lives of more Americans than do those of any other federal agency." He then devolves into outrageous lies about the Trump and Biden administrations and claims HHS has "lost its way" and lays out five goals for the department.

Not surprisingly Goal #1 is "Protecting Life, Conscience, and Bodily Integrity." There is one sentence that is the key take-away: "The Secretary must ensure that all HHS programs and activities are rooted in deep respect for innocent life from day one until natural death: Abortion and euthanasia are not healthcare."

Since the Supreme Court overturned Roe v Wade fourteen states have put abortion bans in place, some with no exception for rape or incest.

Let's put this in the perspective of healthcare costs.

The increased number of children born means increased healthcare, as well as childcare costs for women who may or may not have a second income to rely on or even a job that provides insurance. As for making end-of-life decisions when quality of life is unachievable and suffering is all that is left, the conservative right believes no one has the right to end their own life. Prolonged suffering means increased healthcare costs and more profit for corporations and insurance companies.

Goal #2 "Empowering Patient Choices and Provider Autonomy" applies the economic principle of supply and demand to healthcare costs. It states, "costs tend to decrease, and quality and options tend to increase when there is robust and free competition in the provision of goods and services."

The claim is that healthcare is not an exception to this rule; however, a web search to better understand the supply and demand principle reveals "Demand for basic necessities is relatively inelastic. It's less responsive to changes in their price." Applying economics to healthcare is a win-win for the provider or insurance companies, but not for the consumer.

This goal continues by saying providers should be free to address patient needs, but states should regulate the medical profession. They also want to reduce "burdens of regulatory compliance." We have seen this before in other parts of this document; move everything to the state level with no federal oversight to level the playing field from state to state and strip down regulations that are intended to protect the American people.

Goal #3 is basically an attack on the LGBTQ+ community and single parent households.

Project 2025 wants to remove transgender and non-binary people from existence, at least as far as giving them equality in healthcare. Their statement that "HHS should prioritize married father engagement in its messaging, health, and welfare policies" means their focus will further marginalize those in poor communities and all those children who will be forced to have babies that are a result of rape and incest.

Goal #4 wants to redefine when a pandemic becomes a real healthcare emergency. We all remember COVID-19 and how Trump and the GOP were more concerned with the economy than people. Since the virus appeared in the U.S. there were over one million deaths through May 2023. The Project 2025 plan for the next pandemic may very well triple that amount when the next healthcare crisis appears. Those most at risk will be poor communities and minorities.

The last goal is all about dismantling the National Institutes of Health, Centers for Disease Control and Prevention and the Food and Drug Administration. They call for these critical healthcare offices to get their funding only from the government "with robust congressional oversight."

Project 2025 wants to take science-based decisions out of the hands of scientists. An ultra-conservative Congress who believes in "natural death" will now be deciding when and if a vaccine will be produced for the next viral pandemic and make it optional in schools where those children they forced to be born are now at risk of dying.

Political agendas and even more misinformation would now drive the next crisis.

Centers for Medicare and Medicaid Services (CMS)

Project 2025 refers to Medicare and Medicaid as "runaway entitle-ments that stifle medical innovation, encourage fraud and impede cost con-tainments." The term entitlement is commonly used when it comes to social programs that workers have paid into, so they have something for retirement. They imply an entitlement is a free give away of federal money.

One of the goals for Medicare is to "Increase Medicare beneficiaries' control of their health care." It is clear in this section that Project 2025 knows absolutely nothing about how Medicare works. Their claim that they can make it, so beneficiaries have more choices in doctors, hospitals, and insur-ance plans is ludicrous. We already have all these things with Medicare Parts A and B plus supplemental insurance. What they really want is for private insurance to take complete control of Medicare.

More than half of Medicare recipients participate in the Medicare Part C (Medicare Advantage) plan. Project 2025 wants to make Medicare Part C the "default enrollment option." They not only want everyone covered by for-profit insurance companies, but also to "remove burdensome policies that micromanage MA plans."

Medicare Part C is already a bad idea for people who want or need flexibility in their healthcare providers. It may entice you with the term "all inclusive" or hearing aids and dental are covered, but beneficiaries need to read the fine print and do their homework before signing up. These plans usually have a network where they pay all or almost all costs incurred, such as hospital or doctor visits. If you are out of network, good luck.

When you hear the term "$0 monthly premium" it means your co-pays are high and your annual out of pocket could be $15,000 or more.

The Affordable Care Act (ACA) currently prohibits insurance compa-nies from denying coverage to those with "pre-existing conditions." With Project 2025 this policy will no longer apply and when private insurance controls Medicare they may not deny coverage but will make premiums almost out of reach for some seniors.

You better have a very large 401(k) portfolio if Project 2025 starts fiddling with Medicare.

Medicare Part D, the prescription drug plan is required if patients opt for traditional Medicare Parts A and B. Drugs are included under a Part C plan. Since the Inflation Reduction Act (IRA) was signed by President Joe Biden, insulin has been capped at $35 per month, Medicare will be allowed to negotiate drug prices and in 2025 annual out of pocket costs will be capped at $2,000.

Project 2025 calls for a repeal of the IRA. It seems Project 2025 wants to give beneficiaries choices while doing nothing to control rising costs which come into play when making those choices.

Under the conservative plan, millions of seniors across America will be making the choice of whether to live or die a potentially painful "natural death" because they can't afford treatment or essential drugs. Regarding Medicaid, Project 2025 does not want expansion and South Carolina's governor Henry McMaster says it is a non-starter in his state. Project 2025 feels that reforms, such as work incentives for those who can work and increasing premiums for those with higher incomes is the answer. None of their so-called solutions do anything for nursing home residents who rely on Medicaid for end-of-life care.

The Affordable Care Act and Private Health Insurance

It is no secret that the Republican Party has tried to repeal the Affordable Care Act (ACA) since it first came into being. If it wasn't for the late Sen. John McCain (R-AZ), this critical program would not be available today and 21.3 million people would have no access to affordable healthcare insurance.

The Project 2025 claim that the ACA "has made insurance more expensive and less competitive" is questionable at best. With insurance companies making multi-billion dollar profits every year; it is safe to say that any increased cost is most likely due to corporate greed with the ACA as the scapegoat.

Although the plan does not specifically call for repealing the ACA, it does want to separate the non-subsidized from subsidized market and get rid of regulations for the non-subsidized one. Regulations like the one mentioned above about pre-existing conditions. Here we are again with taking away regulations to protect Americans across every state and allowing corporations the freedom to do whatever they want. This is a common theme across this manifesto for everything in the federal government.

What Can We Do to Stop This?

Implementing the Project 2025 plan will have a detrimental effect on everyone who is struggling even on two incomes and those in poorer communities. Health insurance companies will see even larger profits when they have little or no regulations. Americans on Medicare will be forced into a plan that limits what they currently have under the traditional plans and at higher costs.

The Affordable Care Act, even though it is not really on the chopping block, will be slowly dismantled before being eliminated and leaving millions of people without affordable insurance options.

Trump and the Republicans claimed in 2016 they would replace the ACA with something better. Their plan was just a lot of empty promises, but now with the guidelines from Project 2025 they have a blueprint to work from and it is far from better.

The only way to stop this threat to America's healthcare system is to get out and vote November 5. Kamala Harris and a united Democratic party will always be on the side of all Americans to protect their right to affordable and quality healthcare. Understanding Project 2025 is essential when it comes time to vote.

❖❖❖

Understanding Project 2025: The Blessings of Liberty

By C J Waldron

August 9, 2024

PROMISE #4 SECURE OUR GOD-GIVEN INDIVIDUAL RIGHT TO ENJOY "THE BLESSINGS OF LIBERTY."

The fourth guiding principle of *Project 2025,* called the *Conservative Promise,* lays out the tenets of a White Christian Nationalist country. It swaps out the statement from the Declaration of Independence, that we are entitled to "the Pursuit of Happiness" with "The Pursuit of Blessedness". The implication is that only by being "blessed", which is code for Christian hubris that you are somehow superior to others, can you enjoy the freedoms promised in the Constitution.

Liberty for All

It goes on to declare that the Founding Fathers wanted to bestow the "Blessings of Liberty" on all. Except when the Constitution was adopted, only landed White males were considered worthy of these "blessings". Blacks were considered 3/5 of a person for the purposes of representation only. They were otherwise deemed as property, with no means of enjoying the "blessings" until 1865 when Lincoln enacted the Emancipation Proclamation. Even then, Blacks were denied basic rights until almost one hundred years later, when the Civil Rights Act of 1964 was written into law.

Project 2025 wants to roll back the protections granted by the Civil Rights Act. An ultra Conservative Supreme Court majority has already begun the process by gutting Affirmative Action along with the 1965 Voting Rights Act, which prevented discrimination of citizens' right to vote based on prior servitude, race, belief, color, ethnicity, sex, and age of those who are at least 18 years old. Basically, if voting rights are extended to one group of people, they cannot be denied to other groups of people.

When the 15th Amendment was passed in 1870, several US states activated stricter voting regulations such as literacy tests and a Poll Tax to prevent Blacks from exercising their newly granted right to vote. These were declared illegal by the Voting Rights Act and those states and counties that had enacted such policies were required to obtain preclearance from the Department of Justice before making any changes to their voting requirements.

Republicans sued to have the act repealed numerous times, but it wasn't until 2013, in *Shelby vs Holder,* that the court declared the anti-discrimination clause of the act as being outdated. They claimed such targeted practices, such as a poll tax, were eradicated, and therefore the protections granted were unnecessary.

While it stopped short of declaring the act to be unconstitutional, the court opened the door for other types of restrictions to be enacted. Following Donald Trump's defeat in 2020, several states passed more restrictive voting practices. They used the baseless claims of voter fraud and protecting election integrity to justify enacting these new regulations, which overwhelmingly favored Republican, particularly MAGA, candidates.

These voting restrictions that have been put in place in red states could end up blowing up in their faces. In Florida, restrictions placed on drop off ballot boxes have made it more difficult for their substantial elderly population to vote. Many would be unwilling, or unable, to wait in long lines as Floridians continue to swelter in 90-degree heat, even in November. Other states are reporting similar issues.

Project 2025 wants to continue to create more obstacles to vote for people of color, thereby ensuring Conservatives will maintain their grip on the reins of power. It wants to control who gets to enjoy the "Blessings of Liberty". Could such a strategy cost them the election?

From Sea to Shining Sea

Project 2025 declares that the Founding Fathers wanted to reject the practice of European colonialism "just as we rejected slavery, second-class citizenship for women, mercantilism, socialism, Wilsonian globalism, Fascism, Communism, and (today) wokeism." It completely ignores the policy of *Manifest Destiny* that declared America was to expand from sea to shining sea, as ordained by our Creator, when government sponsored land grabs such as the Oklahoma Land Rush of 1893 rejected established treaties made with Native Americans who had already occupied the territory.

Given their current views on women and people of color, it is with a tremendous amount of *chutzpah* that those involved with Project 2025 can claim credit for abolishing slavery and expanding rights for women. You only have to look at the current Republican presidential ticket to find that assertion laughable.

The Mexican-American War allowed the United States to annex Texas (They can have it back), as well as to purchase California for an amount less than the average major league ballplayer makes. Somehow this is ignored as the act of a colonial power.

Treaties made with the Native American population were routinely disregarded when gold, oil or other natural resources were discovered on land granted to our indigenous population. How is that not colonization?

Those on the Right will almost certainly argue that these things are in the past or are examples of Critical Race Theory. America no longer has any colonial policies.

Except....

There are currently at least 14 territories that are considered US Protectorates (read colonies). Their residents are considered US citizens, but they do not enjoy the same rights as states. They pay taxes but are denied representation. This is the same argument that led to our own American Revolution.

One of the most well-known US territories, Puerto Rico, annexed in 1898 following the Spanish-American War, has repeatedly sought statehood. Donald Trump was mocked for his tactless behavior of throwing paper towels at those on the island recovering from a devastating hurricane. He further compounded his ignorance by claiming to have phoned the President of Puerto Rico following the disaster. Somehow, he was unaware that, at the time, HE was the ruler of the US held territory.

Following the January 6th insurrection, several Republicans pointed to the 1954 attack by Puerto Rican nationalists as justification for the attempted coup.

So, there are several examples of how the United States has not rejected colonialism, both by its past and current behavior. Despite this, *Project 2025* continues to claim America's refusal to be a colonial power is one of the reasons for its "blessed" status in the world.

Teach Your Children...Well?

One of the primary reasons *Project 2025* is able to get their messaging out so effectively is the limited amount of information their base is willing to accept. Their lack of historical knowledge also makes them ripe for manipulation.

On any given day you can find a meme on social media expounding the virtues of going to trade school over getting a college education. According to the authors, government should "promote educational opportunities outside the woke-dominated system of public schools and universities, including trade schools, apprenticeship programs, and student-loan alternatives that fund students' dreams instead of Marxist academics".

While promoting trade schools is admirable, it is the hallmark of every authoritarian regime to belittle the intelligentsia in order to achieve their goals. Hitler, Stalin, Mao, Pol Pot and other dictators have risen to power on the backs of the "poorly educated". Which makes Donald Trump's comment to a Las Vegas crowd during the 2016 primaries all the more chilling.

Those with less education are more likely to believe an authority figure. This makes them more susceptible to being convinced by conspiracy theories. The isolation of COVID gave these outlandish suggestions time to percolate in their minds, making them more like to believe one, then another, until they had gone so far down the rabbit hole of illogic, they were willing to believe anything their side wanted them to.

The comment about "woke public schools "has led to the demonization of educators as groomers of young children, making them easy prey for pedophiles due to their being sexualized by perverse teachers.

Yes, it all sounds ridiculous. Yet, the poorly educated that are the target of *Project 2025's* propaganda campaign are more than willing to accept it as undeniable fact.

Public schools are also the breeding ground for indoctrination. The Woke agenda of Critical Race Theory is promoting a vision of America as lacking greatness. Therefore, it is the duty of every patriotic American to Make America Great Again.

There's your REAL indoctrination for you.

As for colleges being Marxist institutions, it's a fact that authoritarians do not like their actions questioned. Being challenged by those with critical thinking skills is an enormous threat. So, by belittling the educated, it is painting them as being unworthy of enjoying the "blessings of liberty".

Project 2025 is a blueprint for the second Trump administration. It is the 2025 Presidential Transition Project. The four tenets of the project, called the *Conservative Promise* explicitly lay out how they will destroy our system of government.

They are showing us their playbook. Our job is to take action to prevent it from happening.

◆◆◆

Understanding Project 2025: Social Security

By V. Susan Hutchinson

August. 14, 2024

To address the need for a social safety net during the Great Depression, President Franklin D. Roosevelt put together a New Deal for Americans. Part of his plan was the Social Security Act of 1935 to keep older people out of poverty.

Over decades Social Security has had many revisions and become much more complicated than its original concept. With millions of retirees, as well as disabled persons receiving benefits, and with millions more coming to the program in the next ten years, Social Security is inching closer and closer to depletion of funds if nothing is done to prevent it. The Heritage Foundation, responsible for Project 2025, says they have the perfect plan.

How Did Social Security Get into This Situation?

The Social Security Administration (SSA) recently announced benefits would be reduced by 17 percent in 2035 if Congress does not act. This is a slight improvement over their previous expectation of 20 percent in 2033. The Heritage Foundation website claims the deficits began in 2010 under the Obama administration.

This is far from the truth.

The baby boom after World War II plus several expansions to Social Security, which now include payments to disabled workers and to young families who have lost their primary income earner through death, have contributed to its current slide toward insolvency.

The Nixon and Ford administrations were responsible for amendments that created a new program, the Supplemental Security Income (SSI), and implementing an annual cost-of-living increase. This restructure of Social Security immediately led to funding issues and the payroll tax was slightly increased in 1977.

In George W. Bush's first State of the Union address in 2001, he stated that Social Security reform had to be done. He wanted to preserve benefits, make the program more financially sound and offer the option of personal savings accounts to younger workers. At the start of Bush's second term, he was still saying Social Security reform was his top priority.

Bush never accomplished Social Security reform.

The Project 2025 reference to 2010 being the tipping point is based on the American Recovery and Reinvestment Act of 2009, which appropriated money for administrative and information technology needs in SSA. As much as the Heritage Foundation wants to blame President Barack Obama, history has shown there is no one point in time that marks the potential decimation of the Social Security program.

Fiddling With the Retirement Age and Salary Cap

The original age requirement to receive full benefits was 65, but in 1956 an amendment made it possible for women aged 62 to start collecting reduced benefits and in 1961 this option was extended to men. During the Reagan administration, in 1983, full retirement age was raised to 67 for anyone born in or after 1960. In addition, anyone between 62 and 67 who wanted to start collecting would now have their benefits further reduced, while anyone postponing retirement until the age of 70 would see more money in their monthly checks.

This plan was intended to discourage early retirement for those who would be at least partially dependent on Social Security and incentivize people to postpone the receipt of benefits until they reach 70.

This attempt at "reforming" Social Security to ensure funds would be available did not accomplish its goal because, well, here we are 41 years later still trying to keep the program afloat.

The other critical component of Social Security is the wage base or salary cap. This is the maximum salary an employee must earn before they no longer pay Social Security taxes. Over the last ten years there have been several significant increases to the base. In 2014 a person had to make $117,000 or more before they stopped paying.

Today, the base is $168,600 mainly due to two large increases of 9 percent in 2023 and 5.2% in 2024. These increases, under the Biden administration, give Americans an indication of where the Democrats think money should be coming from to put Social Security on a path to solvency.

And it is not the dwindling middle class footing the bill.

The Radical Right Have the Solution

Social Security benefits are distributed from the Old-Age and Survivors Insurance (OASI) Trust Fund, while disability payments come from the Disability Insurance (DI) Trust Fund. Employers and employees both contribute to these trusts, but at different percentages of gross income. Currently, the OASI contribution is based on 5.3 percent from both employer and employee up to the wage cap. The DI is solvent through at least 2097 while the OASI, as stated above, will start running short of funds in 2035 when the SSA will be forced to reduce payouts to keep the program going.

Calls by conservatives for cuts to Social Security are intended to reduce administrative costs, which only account for only 0.4 percent of the OASI budget. House Republicans have proposed a budget that calls for a $450 million cut to SSA administrative costs.

As part of their solution, it appears the Heritage Foundation and House Republicans want to defund the Social Security Administration, all while claiming that their plan will not cut Social Security payments. As OASI sees an ever-widening gap between money coming in and money going out, it is very clear that the GOP Congress just wants a fix to one side of this equation.

The other component of the conservative solution is to, again, raise the retirement age, this time to 69. Does raising the age at which you can collect full benefits add enough money to fill the coffers of the OASI fund?

It does not.

If Reagan's Social Security reform of raising the age worked, we would not be looking at 17 percent reduced benefits in about 10 years. Raising the age people can collect full benefits is an attempt to force Americans to stay in the workforce longer hoping they will die before they can collect the money they paid into the system. And now, younger generations will now have to compete for jobs with millions of more people who would have retired.

Regarding Understanding Project 2025: Social Security, the Heritage Foundation's webpage on Social Security and raising the minimum age makes for an interesting fictional read. They claim Social Security "sought to protect against poverty in old age and to prevent younger generations from bearing the financial burden of that protection." They go on to say today's younger generation bears "100 percent of the program's costs as every dollar of Social Security benefits comes straight out of current workers' paychecks instead of from retirees past payroll taxes."

Sorry, what?

Do they think SSA originally had separate accounts for every person working in America that their taxes went into for retirement? And that you could only collect the exact amount you put in and now this is no longer true? So, raising the retirement age forces you to add more money to "your" account so you have more when you retire instead of using money your grandchildren are contributing. The Heritage Foundation also uses life expectancy to justify why the minimum age needs to be raised and as generations live longer it should be continually adjusted.

There are many questions about the knock-on effect of this plan to the economy and labor, but that is for another day.

The glaring omission from the conservative plan to make SSA solvent is the wage cap. As we all know the GOP and think tanks like the Heritage Foundation are all about making the rich richer at the expense of the working class.

It is not an oversight that they do not want to raise the wage cap higher to bring in enough money to OASI solvent. You don't have to be a mathematician to figure out that increasing the amount coming in is the only sure way to have funds for the future. There is variability as to when people want or need to retire, which may include supplementing their retirement plan with Social Security or if they want to retire earlier than 69 and accept reduced payments. This variability always will affect the money going out part of the equation.

Potential Effects of Not Fixing Social Security Correctly

Most, if not all retirees craft a very careful budget for their last years of life. Some have substantial retirement funds from IRA or 401k accounts and may need very little from Social Security. The latest data from September 2023 shows about 52 million retired persons are collecting Social Security benefits. Half of the people age 65 and older get half of their income from Social Security and 25 percent rely on it for at least 90 percent of their income.

The average monthly benefit is $1918 before deducting Medicare premiums. Medicare increases their premiums annually and the Social Security cost of living increases may or may not cover these added expenses. If they do, there can sometimes be very little increase in monthly Social Security checks.

Retiree budgets can include the high cost of prescriptions if they have conditions, such as diabetes, heart disease or cancer. Housing costs like mortgages or rents and utilities also need to be included when planning for retirement as well as any property taxes.

Any reduction to Social Security payments can mean the difference between surviving and living a quality life. A 17 percent reduction, as proposed for 2035, means only $1592 less the Medicare premium, which will continue to increase every year.

Add inflation or corporate greed into the mix with these reduced benefits and some retirees may have to make decisions on whether they can afford to buy needed medication or food. Before COVID-19 there were already approximately 5.2 million seniors facing food insecurity. The pandemic made it worse.

It is critical for America's future that a long term, final fix to Social Security be implemented as soon as possible.

The final solution is not that envisioned in the Heritage Foundation's plan for 2025. All that plan does is kick the can further down the road and make it another generation's problem.

Franklin Delano Roosevelt would be appalled.

◆◆◆

Understanding Project 2025: Civil Rights

By C J Waldron

Aug. 20, 2024

Ever since President Lyndon Johnson enacted the Civil Rights Act of 1964, Republicans have been trying to undermine it. Voting restrictions, housing discrimination and unfair hiring practices were means of preventing those who needed it most from enjoying the protections the law was intended to provide.

Project 2025 aims at dismantling those protections and replacing them with its "family values" agenda. Using a distorted definition of Critical Race Theory and making Diversity, Equity and Inclusion (DEI) buzzwords for gender radicalism, it proposes eliminating the Office of Civil Rights and re-assigning its purposed duties to the Office of Homeland Security (which it has also suggested closing).

Rather than protecting the rights of minorities, *Project 2025* wants to protect the rights of those who bully the LBGTQ+ population. It claims that the actual rights being violated are those of "hard working Americans" who are often the subject of ridicule for opposing gender dysphoria and the mutilation of our youth.

They assert that the Civil Rights Act has weakened our workforce, in particular our military, by unfair hiring and promotion practices that have allowed a highly qualified White applicant to be passed over in favor of a less qualified minority. They want to eliminate the DEI policies that resulted in these "unfair" labor practices. That is the essence of Project 2025 as it relates to civil rights.

Voting Rights

Occurring in the midst of a global pandemic, the 2020 Presidential

Election demanded some changes be made in the name of keeping the public safe. Despite many of these practices being in place for many years, Republicans who lost elections made unsubstantiated accusations of voter fraud. They demanded, and got, many changes to voter requirements that unfairly targeted minority populations.

Extreme gerrymandering, stricter voter identification requirements, elimination of drop boxes used for mail-in voting, restricting mail-in ballots and closing polling places in minority areas are among the changes imposed by Red States in the name of "preserving voter integrity".

Some states, like Georgia, have even gone as far as to allow one person to challenge an unlimited number of voter registrations. A Texas-based non-profit, True the Vote, has already begun challenging voter rolls based upon conspiracy theories of voter fraud while at least 70 pro–Donald Trump election denialists are working as election officials in key swing states. The net result would be to delay the certification of election results indefinitely if the outcome wasn't to Republican's benefit.

Following the 2020 election, Republicans refused to acknowledge Joe Biden's victory and would respond with the party line "Joe Biden is the president" when queried as to whether they accepted the result. Now they are adopting a similar strategy for the 2024 contest.

When asked if they will accept the results, they now respond with the well-rehearsed comment" I will accept the results of a free and fair election", leaving the door open to protest the outcome should Donald Trump lose. Some, including the primary author of Project 2025, Kevin Roberts, have even suggested a bloody confrontation should Trump lose again.

Project 2025 has outlined measures as to how the Justice Department would aggressively prosecute those suspected of voter fraud. It makes no mention of what needs to be done in cases of voter suppression or intimidation, while the Trump campaign has demanded ballot observers be present to ensure "election integrity".

Diversity, Equity and Inclusion

According to *Project 2025*, there is a Diversity, Equity and Inclusion (DEI) revolution taking place in America. It began with the Obama administration and continues under President Biden. It claims that policies that incorporate DEI standards unfairly discriminate conservatives, those with certain religious beliefs and those who are "pro-life". It proposes eliminating DEI requirements from Federal hiring practices.

The authors of the project want to close the Office of Diversity, Equity and Inclusion, claiming it pushes an undue cost to taxpayers. Closing the office would save $44 million by their estimates.

But then they propose that those funds be used to augment the budget of the Office of the Taxpayer Advocate, so where are the savings they actually use as justification?

With Kamala Harris as the Democratic nominee, Republicans have been quick to jump on the bandwagon denouncing DEI policies and even smearing Harris's accomplishments by calling her a "DEI hire". They completely ignore the fact she was duly elected as district attorney, attorney general and senator based upon her performance and not her race or gender.

Diversity is essential in policymaking decisions. Otherwise, the will of one race or gender would overrule resolutions that could have a profound impact on those who are forced to accept a biased ruing. A prime example is the *Dobbs* decision overturning abortion rights. With the choice being left to the individual states, all-White predominantly male legislators are forcing their beliefs onto women without permitting their input.

Equity is the practice of providing equal pay for equal work. It also means equal treatment when it comes to hiring and firing. *Project 2025* wants to include loyalty to Donald Trump as a requirement for keeping your civil service position. The authors want to eliminate racial classifications which they consider to be a form of discrimination under Title VII of the Civil Rights Act of 1964. The act protects job applicants and employees from employment discrimination based on race, color, religion, sex, or national origin. Yet, they want to change the language to delete any mention of race as a qualification.

Inclusion means that those with a disabling condition would not have that used as a disqualifying factor when it comes to federal hiring practices. While *Project 2025* does not explicitly state that it is unwilling to provide accommodations, it does demand that the National Institute for Health close the Office of Diversity, Equity and Inclusion. This would eliminate a vital avenue for those with disabilities to lodge complaints regarding workplace discrimination.

According to authors of *Project 2025*, inclusion also means being forced to accept a person's preferred sexual identity. They further claim that it somehow leads to the proliferation of child pornography due to someone's "unnatural" sexual proclivities.

Project 2025 declares that DEI is nothing less than the promotion of the "Woke" agenda which aims at weakening America by forcing it to accept less qualified candidates for important political positions. It asserts that gender ideology should not be a consideration when it comes to hiring or firing practices.

Critical Race Theory

A major weapon in curtailing Civil Rights is the promotion of the idea that Critical Race Theory is indoctrinating our children to hate America. MAGA Republicans have promoted entire campaigns with the promise of eliminating Critical Race Theory from the classroom.

The problem is it was never in the classroom in the first place. What they term Critical Race Theory is actually a truthful examination of American history. Studying slavery, the Trail of Tears or Japanese Internment during

World War II have been called Critical Race Theory because they describe an America that is not the "Shining City on the Hill" espoused by Ronald Reagan and other political figures.

As a part of the Federal government, *Project 2025* wants to eliminate Marxist indoctrination and divisive critical race theory programs and make anyone who promotes such ideas to be grounds for immediate dismissal.

The problem is by ignoring the issues of our past, we allow them to be committed again. Trump has already proposed setting up internment camps for illegal immigrants, should he win re-election.

What's to stop him from further taking away the civil rights Americans fought to attain? The idyllic version of a return to the 1950s style of America, when racial discrimination, sexual harassment, segregated schools and housing and voter suppression was a way of life, is what *Project 2025* embraces.

◆◆◆

Understanding Project 2025: The Environment

By V. Susan Hutchinson

August 24, 2024

We learned very quickly in 2020 during the COVID-19 pandemic that Donald J. Trump and the Republican Party care absolutely nothing for the health and safety of people across the country. Project 2025 lays out exactly how much farther they are willing to go to inflict long term harm on the health of the American people with their policies on protecting, or rather not protecting the environment.

According to the Department of Health and Human Services, over 12 million people worldwide die due to environmental pollution. In the United States we can expect an increase in respiratory and cardiac diseases as well as some cancers if the conservatives get their hands on the Environmental Protection Agency (EPA).

Lies, Hypocrisy and Looking Out for Corporate America

Kevin Roberts, in the forward to Project 2025, claims that the federal government is "growing larger and less constitutionally accountable – even to the President." This is probably the biggest lie in the entire document.

As an example of this lack of accountability, he claims the EPA is strangling domestic energy production. The truth is that under President Joe Biden, energy production is at an all-time high. Is this contradictory to our claim America should be using clean energy? Not at all. We know that the short-term need for oil and gas production must be addressed as we move to the long-term goal of clean energy.

The conservatives will have you believe the Democrats will leave everyone in the lurch and switch America to clean energy without warning.

Another big lie in Roberts' forward is the statement "The next conservative President must possess the courage to relentlessly put the interests of the everyday American over the desires of the ruling elite." Could someone from the Heritage Foundation please explain how Trump's quid pro quo to big oil puts the interests of "everyday Americans" first?

The Project 2025 plan for "creating a better environmental tomorrow with clean air, safe water, healthy soil and thriving communities" is just a bunch of words thrown together to distract from the real purpose, which is to remove or drastically revise policies that protect the health of Americans and strip regulations so corporations can increase their already enormous profits.

Although Project 2025 does not call for eliminating the EPA, this doctrine targets multiple offices and programs, as well as Biden's successful Inflation Reduction Act (IRA) of 2022.

Project 2025 claims the EPA has been "reimagined in an attempt to expand the reach of the federal government."

As with goals defined for various other federal agencies, Project 2025 wants to give states more control of environmental protections. With the help of the Supreme Court, the EPA's authority is already being eroded. This recent ruling says the federal government cannot dictate that states protect the rights to clean air of individuals in surrounding states. This "Good Neighbor Program/Interstate pollutant transport" program is specifically called out for repeal in the section on the Office of Air and Radiation (OAR).

The Heritage Foundation has already checked this one off their list even before Trump reclaims power.

Dismissing the Need for Federal Regulations

Destroying standards that have a national, and possibly global effect means conservatives can force their anti-environment policies on everyone. We have seen in other sections of this document, most notable the Department of Education, that the ultra-conservative minority believes everyone should live by their rules. Throwing every American's right to life, liberty and the pursuit of happiness out the window is their ultimate goal.

Examples of their disdain for federal regulations include establishing car standards that would consider cost and choice, stopping the increase in standards for airplanes under the International Civil Aviation Organization and reconsidering the Cleaner Trucks Initiative so decreasing emissions does not create "complex burdens on the industry."

The Heritage Foundation is all about reducing the cost to industries and any detrimental effect on those "everyday Americans" is acceptable risk that needs to be taken.

A Variety of Damaging Reforms

Office of Water (OW)

The Clean Water Act (CWA) is a particular target of Project 2025. The intent of the CWA is to "give states and authorized tribes the authority to grant, deny or waive certification of proposed federal licenses or permits that may discharge into waters off the United States." Among other things, Project 2025 wants a clear definition of what is a United States waterway in context of private property rights, claiming OW regulations currently infringe on these rights.

Their plan for the OW is to "reform the guidance on guidance." They want guidance documents to be clearly intended as guidance, which means "they do not have the effect of law and should not be treated by the office as if they did have any such effect." Project 2025 wants clear rules and definitions, enforced time limits and requirements for regulations covered under the CWA. They also want to shift employees to other programs and out to regional offices.

It sounds very much like they don't really want guidelines, but their set of strict rules pushed out to the state level when it comes to waterways.

Office of Land and Emergency Management (OLEM)

The mission of OLEM is to establish guidelines for the disposal of hazardous waste, establish safe waste management practices for all levels of government including waste reduction and recycling, support of state programs to redevelop contaminated sites so they could be reused and encouragement of technology development to clean up contaminated soil and groundwater.

If you do not know what perflouornonanoic acid (PFNA) and polyfluoroalkyl substances (PFAS) are you need to educate yourself now. PFNA is found in carpets, food-contact paper and cleaning products that have been sold to consumers for decades. They resist heat, water and chemicals and remain in the environment forever as they do not degrade. The EPA's Integrated

Risk Information System (IRIS) has designated PFAS as hazardous substances.

Project 2025 wants to "revisit the designation of PFAS and its associated chemicals as hazardous substances under CERCLA." CERCLA is the Comprehensive Environmental Response, Compensation and Liability Act responsible for not only clean-up of inactive hazardous sites, but for costs to those transporting hazardous substances and on current or former owners of those facilities. CERCLA gives authority to the President of the United States to respond to the release or threat of release of hazardous substances into our environment.

Revisiting, in the context of the Project 2025 doctrine, means they want to remove the hazardous label for PFAS and its related substances and make sure the President cannot impede or stop production of products that contain these chemicals.

In March of 2024, well after Project 2025 was published, the EPA requested a toxicology review of PFNA. The executive summary states "this assessment concludes that the evidence demonstrates that oral exposure to PFNA causes developmental effects in humans, and that the evidence indicates that oral exposure to PFNA is likely to cause hepatic and male reproductive effects in humans given sufficient exposure conditions."

It identifies exposure to PFNA as being associated with low birth weights.

Does anyone think the Heritage Foundation will now change their mind on PFAS? It is not very likely. Once they open the door to "revisit" this hazardous material designation, it paves the way for stripping that designation from other materials used in manufacturing.

In addition, Project 2025 calls for conducting new chemical evaluations in the context of "competitiveness of U.S. manufacturers" and revising regulations for new chemical review.

As Cheryl M. Cail, Acting Chief of the Waccamaw Indian People states,

"There is a plan to set things up so that manufacturers can move through the use of new chemicals with even less review."

As if paving the way for increasing consumer exposure to hazardous chemicals is not enough, Project 2025 calls for transferring the EPA Safer Choice program to the "private sector". The Safer Choice label on products lets people know an independent assessment was made on the product for their protection. Making manufacturers now responsible for appropriately labeling their product means they can now get a product cleared without all the previous red tape and testing and label it "safe."

Would you believe anything a manufacturer tells you about the safety of their product knowing that their only interest is profit and not your family's life?

Looking Out for the Health and Safety of Your Family

Project 2025 is the blueprint for a Trump presidency. In 2010 Citizens United designated corporations as "people" and made it legal for them to buy political influence with large campaign contributions. Many of the bills proposed in Congress are often drafted by lobbyists for political interests, not the people's representatives.

When it comes to protection of the environment, which affects every living thing on the planet, corporations will always choose their interests first and use political influence to clear the way for increased profits.

The right to clean air and water with very limited exposure to toxic chemicals should always be federally controlled.

The writers of Project 2025 claim to be experts on every government agency they want to reform or eliminate. When it comes to our environment and health, their ideas are hazardous to all Americans, which is why understanding Project 2025: the Environment is so critical.

To look out for our own safety and keep the conservative minority from exposing us to an unhealthy environment, we need to exercise our right to vote and put Representatives, Senators and a President in power who will have our backs and protect not only the health of all Americans, but our planet as well.

Vote Blue up and down the ticket as it will take not only a Democratic President to keep us safe, but a Democratic House and Senate and local offices as well.

◆◆◆

Understanding Project 2025: Reshaping the Federal Workforce

By C J Waldron

September 1, 2024

One of the key aims of *Project 2025* is to reshape the federal workforce by either eliminating certain positions or replacing career federal workers with Trump loyalists.

It uses the rationale that it is a budget saving move, while in actuality it is nothing more than a coup on the federal bureaucracy in order to strengthen the Trump administration's stranglehold on Washington.

Schedule F

Because of its unpopularity, Trump has sought to distance himself from *Project 2025*, yet he cannot deny that reshaping the federal workforce was going to be a crucial piece of his second administration, had he won re-election in 2020. Prior to Election Day that year he issued an Executive Order, Schedule F, which aimed to do that very thing.

139

Under Schedule F, government employees could be more easily fired, re-assigned, or let go simply because their position had been eliminated. For example, those employed by the Department of Veterans Affairs, those who handle issues dealing with veterans, would be replaced by chat bots.

In keeping with Trump's "I love the poorly educated", *Project 2025* proposes making more federal appointments based upon skills rather than having an education requirement. This would make it easier to justify hiring someone less qualified based upon their loyalty to Trump rather than their knowledge of vital information such as specific legal issues.

Because Schedule F had already been enacted prior to Election Day, Trump would have been free to dismiss thousands of federal employees the moment he was declared the victor. *Project 2025* wants to grant him that ability once again should he win in November. It wants to prohibit the use of a BA requirement in job postings.

Diversity, Equity and Inclusion

Programs promoting Diversity. Equity and Inclusion (DEI) have been in place to prevent discrimination in federal hiring practices. Under DEI, a prospective employee could no longer be denied a position based upon their race, gender or sexual preferences.

This has outraged the White Christian nationalists who contend that such a policy is not in keeping with their interpretation of the Founding Father's intent to create a Christian nation.

Project 20205 contends that DEI hiring practices have resulted in more highly qualified candidates being passed over due to the demand that a person of color or a certain gender must be included in specific federal agencies. Republican lawmakers have even gone as far as to label Democratic presidential front-runner Kamal Harris "a DEI hire".

Project 2025 also asserts that requiring employees to attend workshops on DEI policies is a poor use of their time. Forcing Pentagon employees to undergo such training is an ineffective use of their resources and unproductive to their role as military personnel, the proposal contends.

Despite his denials, the similarities between Schedule F and *Project 2025* are impossible to ignore. Should Donald Trump become president once again, it would create a federal bureaucracy that would allow him to yield limitless power over all branches of government, including the military.

Project 2025 wants to make it easier for federal employees to be fired simply for being gay. It wants to revisit the *Bostock* decision where an employee who worked for Clayton County, Georgia was fired for joining a gay softball league.

Writing for the majority, conservative Justice Neal Gorsuch ruled that Bostock's rights were protected under Title VII of the Civil Rights Act of 1964. It did so on a plain language reading of the statute, a judicial philosophy known as textualism. Justice Gorsuch was joined by one other Republican-appointed justice, John Roberts, and the four Democratic-appointed justices.

Now, with a new Trump-appointed set of justices, those involved with *Project 2025* hope to reverse this ruling, allowing it to be extended to federal workers. In essence, they want to go back to a time when people could be blackmailed for being part of the LBGTQ community. They want to force them to go "back in the closet:". Those who do not conform to their definition of the binary biological definition of sex would be denied any protections from discrimination.

Further evidence that *Project 2025* is the product of White Christian Nationalists is the proposed extension of religious protections for those who would be exempted from working on the Sabbath. The exemption would default to Sundays, but those with "sincere" religious beliefs would also be allowed.

So basically, if you are a Christian, you get a free pass, but if you are Jewish, you need a note from your rabbi?

Many Project 2025 Federal Workforce proposals are truly Draconian provisions that claim to support their *Conservative Promise.* It wants to roll back protections for Federal workers by making it easier to fire certain employees if they fail to conform to their standards.

We cannot allow this to happen.

◆◆◆

Chapter Four

The Biden Legacy

When Joe Biden was running for President, he said he was fighting to restore the soul of America. He did his best in the face of great odds, and in the process achieved a great deal. Then, age caught up with him and in July 2024, he stepped aside in favor of Vice President Kamala Harris. As Americans, we owe him much gratitude.

Biden Goes Big, Republicans Act Like Toddlers

By Bob Gatty

April 29, 2021

Republicans apparently can't stand the fact that President Biden is boldly dealing with the major problems that face us today and that the American people appreciate his efforts.

While the president, since his inauguration, has gone big with bold and successful initiatives to get the Covid 19 pandemic under control and provide critically needed financial resources to those whose lives have been upended by the virus, Republicans are nitpicking, whining, and doing everything they can to sow division and distrust.

Seems like that's all they have.

During Biden's joint address to Congress last night, Sen. Ted Cruz (R-TX), one of the slimiest of all GOP slimeballs, was caught by the TV cameras nodding off and dozing as the president discussed immigration and the problems at our Southern border -- a topic about which Cruz has railed.

But the senator later tweeted that he dozed because Biden's speech was "boring but radical." That makes no sense. If something is radical, how could it be boring? Anyway, Twitter exploded with the video above.

When Biden talked about the need to stop the proliferation of weapons of war that are being used in mass shootings, some Republicans simply shook their heads, while others snickered. His earnest call for the Senate to pass the House-passed For the People Act voting rights bill drew the same reaction.

Those Republican senators chuckled even as mass shootings continue in our nation and as two House-passed bills designed to improve background checks to keep guns out of the hands of potential killers are stuck in their chamber. Republicans hold 50 votes and can block virtually any legislation by using the filibuster, which requires 60 votes to break.

Meanwhile, the House-passed voting rights legislation languishes in the Senate as well, also because of the filibuster. This, of course, is the case as state after Republican state enacts new laws designed to restrict voting in a variety of ways, all in response to Trump's continued unfounded claims that he lost the election due to voter fraud.

Sen. Jim Clyburn (D-SC), whose primary election endorsement of Biden helped him secure the Democratic presidential nomination, says the House-passed bill "advanced the biggest set of voting protections since the Voting Rights Acts of 1965. Georgia's new restrictive law and others like it "are the new Jim Crow," Clyburn says.

As for the Republicans?

Following Biden's speech, Sen. Tim Scott (R-SC), the only Black Republican in the Senate, gave the GOP's response to Biden's address. I thought he was pathetic.

"President Biden promised you a specific kind of leadership. He promised to unite a nation, to lower the temperature, to govern for all Americans, no matter how we voted," Scott said. "But three months in, the actions of the president and his party are pulling us further apart."

Really? Why? Because Biden wants the wealthy and corporations to help finance infrastructure and education improvements, and other initiatives that are designed to benefit everyone, not just the well-to-do?

If Biden's actions are widening, not narrowing divisions, Sen. Scott, why is it that the most recent FiveThirtyEight compilation of polls shows that 53.9 percent of the American people approve of the job he is doing compared to just 38.7 percent for Donald Trump at the 100-day mark of his presidency?

Over Biden's first 100 days he has demonstrated the competence and stability that was sorely lacking in the Trump administration. While the Covid 19 vaccinations were developed during Trump's presidency, it has been under Biden that more than 200 million shots have been given, double the new president's original promise. Now, said Biden, America is "working again, dreaming again, discovering again and leading the world again."

And while the results of those efforts have generated renewed confidence among a majority of Americans, Republicans still look for every way possible to belittle Biden, Vice President Kamala Harris, and his administration. Even if they have to make it up.

House Minority Leader Kevin McCarthy (R-CA) previewed the GOP attacks on Fox News on Sunday, accusing Biden of a "bait and switch" — promising to be a leader who values bipartisanship, but who in actuality passed a $2 trillion pandemic relief bill with no Republican support.

"The bait was he was going to govern as bipartisan, but the switch is he's governed as a socialist," McCarthy said.

Senate Minority Leader Mitch McConnell (R-KY) accused Biden and Democrats of engaging in "brazen misdirection" and living "in an alternate universe where both the campaign promises they made and the mandate the American people delivered were completely different than what happened here on planet Earth."

"Behind President Biden's familiar face, it's like the most radical Washington Democrats have been handed the keys, and they're trying to speed as far left as they can possibly go before American voters ask for their car back," McConnell said. So, what do the Republicans have? Not much, just their tired old tropes, name calling, and efforts to turn the facts around to suit their failed arguments.

Just Plain Silliness

They are also resorting to silliness and, like their master, Trump, bald faced lies.

Conservatives on social media went nuts over a *New York Post* story this past week that claimed undocumented minors were being welcomed to the United States with copies of a children's book written by Vice President Harris and that Harris was making money off of that.

But then the reporter who wrote the story acknowledged that it was a lie, fabricated, made up, and that she had been ordered to do so by her bosses at the right-wing publication owned by Rupert Murdoch, who also owns Fox News.

"The Kamala Harris story — an incorrect story I was ordered to write and which I failed to push back hard enough against — was my breaking point," Laura Italiano tweeted Tuesday afternoon, several hours after her viral article about the books had been deleted from the Post's website and replaced with corrected versions. Italiano resigned from her job as a result.

Meanwhile, conservative lawmakers and GOP party officials jumped all over the story during the four days it remained online and uncorrected.

Sen. Tom Cotton of Arkansas and Rep. Jim Jordan of Ohio both blasted it. And Republican National Committee chair Ronna McDaniel tweeted: "After learning officials are handing out Kamala Harris' book to migrants in facilities at the border, it's worth asking . . . Was Harris paid for these books? Is she profiting from Biden's border crisis?"

Where's the Meat?

That, of course was not the only bit of nastiness cooked up by the Republicans over the past week or so.

There was the stupidly false claim that to fight climate change Biden plans to reduce red meat consumption by 90 percent, limiting everyone to just four pounds of red meat a year.

It all began with a story in the right-wing Daily Mail in the United Kingdom about a University of Michigan study that had nothing to do with any administration initiative. Then, Fox Business host Larry Kudlow warned viewers that there would be "no burgers on July 4th."

Texas Gov. Greg Abbott, Idaho Gov. Brad Little and former South Carolina governor Nikki Haley, all Republicans, jumped on the bandwagon, and Rep. Marjorie Taylor Greene (Ga.) tweeted a picture of Biden with a hamburger to suggest that he was a hypocrite: "No burgers for thee, but just for me."Finally, Fox News's John Roberts apologized for a network graphic that had suggested Biden intended to cut red meat consumption, admitting "that is not the case." That incident and the one about the vice-president's children's book, simply illustrates the fact that Republicans learned well from Trump about the effectiveness of the lie.

As *The Washington Post* reported, the nation experienced 30,573 false or misleading claims over Trump's four years in office, culminating in the baseless claim that the 2020 election was stolen, which ultimately helped provoke the deadly Jan. 6 insurrection at the U.S. Capitol -- and which has spawned all of those GOP bills to prevent people from voting.

What else do the Republicans have these days?

Not much.

◆◆◆

Impeach Joe Biden?

By C J Waldron

August 29, 2021

After the deadly airport attack, there were renewed calls for President Biden to be removed from office. Yes, you heard it right. The very same Republicans who refused to hold Donald Trump responsible for the January 6th insurrection are demanding that President Biden resign of face impeachment.

The hypocrisy is astounding!

They completely ignore that the process of ending American involvement in Afghanistan was initiated by Donald Trump during his chaotic administration. Trump negotiated a peace deal with the Taliban, which has been declared a terrorist organization, without including the recognized Afghan government. This disregarded the longstanding policy that America does not negotiate with terrorists. It also was a slap in the face of Afghan allies who undoubtably felt abandoned by Americans with whom they fought side-by-side for the past two decades.

Despite this, it's President Biden's head that Republicans want on a platter.

In addition to calls for Biden's impeachment or resignation, one South Carolina state representative has even gone as far as to suggest that Biden appoint Donald Trump to oversee the withdrawal of American combat troops from Afghanistan. Russell Fry (R), a member of the South Carolina House of Representatives, said President Biden should appoint Trump "in a spirit of true bipartisanship".

It's enough to make your head explode!

As the chaotic exit from Afghanistan developed, the calls for President Biden's impeachment grew. At the forefront was the man who's his lips are firmly planted on the orange one's derrière, Sen. Lindsey Graham (R-SC). Graham took to the airwaves of right wing media to declare that "Biden deserves to be impeached " if every Afghan ally isn't rescued from the war-torn nation. What an astonishing turn of events, given his staunch approval for Trump during BOTH impeachment trials.

Today, on CBS' Face the Nation, Graham repeated that call, saying Biden was guilty of "dereliction of duty".

Graham is joined by fellow ass-kisser, House Minority Leader Kevin McCarthy (R-CA) in calling for Biden to step down following the disorderly Afghan withdrawal. McCarthy's political ambitions are well known. He wants to reclaim the House Speaker's gavel and has even "joked" that he would use the gavel to attack current House Speaker Nancy Pelosi, should this happen.

Not to be outdone, the man who cheered on the insurrectionists, Sen. Josh Hawley (R-MO), joined by Sen. Marsha Blackburn (R-TN), not only demanded Joe Biden resign or face impeachment, but also declared the same fate should befall Vice President Kamala Harris, Secretary of State Anthony Blinken, Secretary of Defense Lloyd Austin and Joint Chiefs Chairman Mark Miley, following the deadly attacks at the Kabul airport.

Republican desire to impeach Joe Biden predates even his inauguration. Iowa's Joni Ernst (R-IO) stated that Biden should be impeached as far back as February 2020, almost a year before the election and even before Biden decided to enter the presidential race. She cited Biden's alleged involvement in some vague conspiracy with Ukraine as her reason to level charges at the yet undeclared candidate.

QAnon kook Marjorie Taylor Greene (R-GA) introduced articles of impeachment the day following President Biden's inauguration. When the supposed uprising, known as "The Storm", which promised a triumphant return to power of the defeated Donald Trump, failed to materialize, Greene sought to have these same unproven charges of Ukrainian involvement while he was Vice President presented as proof that Biden was unfit for office.

She sought impeachment hearings again on August 20th of this year, citing the "border crisis", the COVID-related eviction moratorium and his handling of the withdrawal in Afghanistan as reasons for this round of hearings that she was assured would end with either Biden's removal or resignation.

The revenge-minded right has been looking for any misstep by the Biden administration. They continue to spread the Big Lie while claiming the dual impeachment trials were politically motivated. They echo the cries of "Witch Hunt" while refusing to investigate Donald Trump's role in the January 6th insurrection.

While the crisis in Afghanistan will surely fade, the demands that Biden be impeached will continue. The pettiness of the petulant politicians on the right won't allow them to let it go. And neither will Donald Trump as he continues to dispute the results of the 2020 election.

Give me a break!!

❖❖❖

Biden Afghanistan: An Act of Courage

By Bob Gatty

September 1, 2021

President Joe Biden has been taking a lot of incoming flak from critics, Republicans, nattering nabobs in the rightwing media, and even some members of his own party for America's rather messy exit from the war-that-would-never-end, Afghanistan.

Here's what I say.

Those who sit on the sidelines and bash him for what he's done need to shut up.

Yes, the execution of the withdrawal was messy, but how could it not be? Not only did the U.S. have to deal with the Taliban, thousands of Afghans clamoring to get out, and terrorist attacks by ISIS-K, they did it against a deadline and in the middle of the Covid-19 pandemic.

And that's probably just the tip of the iceberg.

As former Biden critic Mehdi Hasan said in an opinion piece on MSNBC, "Yet as of Tuesday evening, Biden has done something that three previous presidents either wouldn't or couldn't: ended the longest war in American history. The last U.S. troops left Afghanistan on schedule and ahead of the 20th anniversary of the 9/11 attacks."

And then, Hasan wrote this: Biden "stood up to the generals."

Hasan wrote that in 2017, Donald Trump wanted to wind down the war in Afghanistan, but national security adviser H.R. McMaster wanted him to do the opposite -- send in more troops. So, McMaster apparently played to Trump's penchant for sexy women and reportedly presented him "with a black-and-white snapshot from 1972 of Afghan women in miniskirts walking through Kabul, to show him that Western norms had existed there before and could return."

It worked, wrote Hasan, adding, "Trump, who before entering the White House had called the war a "total disaster" and said the U.S. "should leave Afghanistan immediately," agreed to escalate troop levels."

Previously, Hasan noted, President Obama, at the urging of his generals, signed off on sending 30,000 more U.S. troops to Afghanistan. That came after Vice President Biden, according to Obama's memoir, urged the president "Don't let them jam you," speaking of his generals.

Now, Hasan added, that while Biden after being elected President could have scrubbed the February 2020 agreement Trump signed with the Taliban to withdraw all forces this year, he didn't. He could have listened to his military advisers who wanted him to keep 2,500 troops in Afghanistan, but he didn't do that either.

"Biden didn't let them "jam" him," Hasan wrote. Instead, he announced that all U.S. troops would be gone by Sept. 11, 2021.

Then, of course, came the Taliban's fast takeover, with Afghanistan's president running for cover and chaos erupting in and around the Kabul airport, including the ISIS-K attack that claimed the lives of 13 American troops. The howls from his critics grew louder.

As David Smith wrote in The Guardian, "For Republicans it was a day of thoughts and prayers – and political opportunity."

Smith added, "But Republicans smell blood, having until now struggled to find an effective line of attack against Biden as candidate or president. Although foreign policy rarely decides US elections, the critiques have fueled a pre-existing narrative that the 78-year-old does not have "the right stuff"."

For now, at least, the GOP attacks on the president appear to be working, as his approval rating is dropping and there are calls for his resignation, while Sen. Lindsey Graham (R-SC) and others call for his impeachment.

But the bottom line is this More than 100,000 people were evacuated from Afghanistan since mid-August, including all but 100 or so U.S. citizens who wanted to leave. The critics say Biden and his people should have prepared better, that the evacuation was sloppy at best, catastrophic at worst.

Perhaps.

Nevertheless, Biden made good on his promise, and we are out of Afghanistan, a quagmire that has cost thousands of American lives and trillions of U.S. taxpayer dollars, all for a mission that was doomed from the beginning.

Said President Biden the day after Kabul fell, "How many more generations of America's daughters and sons would you have me send to fight Afghans — Afghanistan's civil war when Afghan troops will not? How many more lives — American lives — is it worth? How many endless rows of headstones at Arlington National Cemetery?"

President Biden promised to get America out of Afghanistan and end that 20-year war. He kept his promise. And for that, he deserves great credit.

◆ ◆ ◆

Biden Needs to Be a Leader

By C J Waldron

October 29, 2021

Another deadline is looming for Joe Biden's economic agenda. And before he left for Europe, he met with Democrats in Congress to hammer out the details and seek passage of two bills that define his presidency. Yet, for weeks the ambitious Build Back Better bill and the bipartisan Infrastructure Investment and Jobs Act have been held hostage by bickering Democratic factions.

On one side you have Senators Joe Manchin (D-WV) and Kysten Sinema (D-UT), who have been whittling the cost of the bill down to exclude certain provisions they found unfavorable. On the other a group calling themselves Progressives; a group of 95 Democrats in the House of Representatives and one Democratic senator. Between them, they have ground President Biden's agenda to a screeching halt.

Biden has held numerous meetings, negotiated, cajoled and compromised in order to get these bills passed. Each time House Speaker Nancy Pelosi (D-CA) refused to bring it to the House floor because she knew she lacked the votes to guarantee passage of both pieces of legislation. Either those on the Senate side refused, where Democrats hold a slim majority, would object to certain provisions, thus guaranteeing the measure would fail, or Progressives would insist that they wouldn't go along unless both were passed in tandem.

Like his predecessor, Biden sees himself as a master deal maker. Unlike the former resident of Pennsylvania Avenue, Biden prefers compromise over bullying. Yet, with each passing day, and lack of progress, Biden is watching his approval ratings drop due to his inability to close the desk on his signature agenda items.

Not only does this make Biden appear weaker, but it also gives Republicans fodder as they aim to retake both the House and Senate during the 2022 midterm elections. So, Manchin, et al aren't doing Democrats, or themselves, any favors by refusing to pass these bills. They are only giving air to the nickname the "Do Nothing Democrats" that was bestowed upon them during the Trump administration.

It's time for Joe Biden to stop compromising and start leading. Instead of caving to the demands of a few stubborn members of his party, he needs to use the power of his office to ensure the will of the majority is heard. Threaten to withhold DNC funding, start looking for opponents to challenge them come re-election time and abandon the filibuster, which has been used by Republicans to stymie efforts by Democrats when they are in the minority.

Despite their numerous flaws, the Republicans have one thing Democrats lack: unity. It is a unity borne out of fear; fear that they will face retaliation if they don't toe the party line. It's a tactic Biden should selectively emulate when push comes to shove. Otherwise, he will have bill after bill held up, not by a filibuster, but by those within his own party who seek to push their own private agendas.

Biden needs to become a leader.

◆◆◆

Pushing Biden on Climate Change 'Code Red'

By Bob Gatty

Jan 17, 2022

President Biden famously said that the world faces a "Code Red" climate crisis and has pledged to make fighting that crisis a top priority of his administration. But is he matching his actions with his words?

Our guest on The Lean to the Left Podcast is Karen Igou, an organizer of a week-long protest over the Christmas holiday called OccupyBiden. It was a 24/7 outdoors Climate Justice Occupation within a mile of President Biden's house in Wilmington, DE.

I found it interesting that such a demonstration would be held targeting Biden, especially considering the harm done by his predecessor, Donald Trump, with his actions that were rooted in the denial of climate change. After all, Biden has been working to reverse many of those actions.

However, many climate activists believe there is more rhetoric than action coming out of the Biden administration, and so some 200 demonstrators from 10 states participated in the OccupyBiden event.

Not only do they say there is more talk than action when it comes to taking action to counteract the forces of climate change, they contend that some of Biden's actions actually have been harmful.

That includes reopening of oil and gas leasing in the Gulf of Mexico, an action that Igou contends was "unnecessary" and "purely political." The action flies in the face of Biden's climate agenda, as he has promised to slash greenhouse gas emissions in half by 2030. Environmental advocates say it could set U.S. climate goals back for years.

"Our demands are that he declare a climate emergency and that his administration grant no new permits for fossil fuel projects," Igou says, noting that even the fossil-friendly International Energy Agency has said this is absolutely necessary to avoid catastrophe.

The group's goal was to present Biden with a letter setting forth those demands and giving him a January 31 deadline to meet them, but the Secret Service guarding the Biden's home would not accept the letter. So, it was read aloud. Marchers then led a single-file line to the security barricade to each leave a flower, intending to appeal to the humanity of the officers and the President. Some chose to take a knee and moment of silence to communicate their message.

Occupy Biden participants say the movement will continue until their demands are met. They have built a strong coalition of concerned citizens and organizations and if their demands are not met by 1/31/22, a larger and more organized event will be planned.

"We are not OK with politics as usual running things," Igou says. "It's not working. We are going in the wrong direction. At least we're trying to address our crisis. We're trying to wake people up. We're trying to get the voices of the people unified to take care of our one and only planet. Our own president has said that we are in a Code Red existential crisis."

She adds, "It's madness. It's lunacy to destroy the very part of the ecosystem that make it work. No other species has ever done what we're doing, which is destroying our own home. We're literally committing ecocide and it's madness."

Igou dedicates her life, and her business, a farm-to-table grocery called Honeybee Kitchen and Market, to fighting the climate crisis. On the podcast, she suggests many ways that you can also get involved to save Mother Earth.

Organizations participating in the OccupyBiden event included:

- 2021 Grandparents Walk for their Grandchildren and Mother Earth
- Beyond Extreme Energy
- Build Back Fossil Free
- Extinction Rebellion DE, Philly, Richmond VA and NYC
- Sunrise DE and Baltimore
- Fridays for Future DE
- Working Families Party
- Honeybee Kitchen and Market
- Democratic Socialists of America
- Climate Mobilization
- Philly Water Protectors
- Seeds of Peace Catering
- Marcellus Outreach Butler (PA) aka MOB
- The Green Party of Butler and Venango Counties
- Code Pink
- Peace, Justice, Sustainability NOW!
- YES Youth Environmental Summit

◆◆◆

Joe Biden's Blind Spot

By C J Waldron

June 5, 2022

Any time Joe Biden introduces a piece of legislation, he exposes his glaring blind spot. He does so with the hope of bipartisan support. Republicans have repeatedly made it abundantly clear that they have zero interest in doing anything that would create positive numbers for Biden, no matter the views of a majority of Americans.

When President Biden took office, he declared he was going to usher in a new era of bipartisanship that was largely absent during the previous administration. Republicans had other ideas. Instead, Mitch McConnell stated he is "100 percent" opposed to the Biden agenda. Like he tried with President Obama, McConnell wants to make Biden a one-term president.

Yet, any time Biden hints he might go it alone, on such things as the Infrastructure Act, Republicans are quick to whine that he is reneging on his promise to be bipartisan. Means of overcoming Republican roadblocks, namely abandoning the filibuster, have been met with opposition from two members of his own party, West Virginia's Joe Manchin and Arizona's Kyrsten Sinema.

When the suggestion of harsher gun control, in the face of the attacks in Buffalo, NY and Uvalde, TX sparked public outrage, McConnell initiated bipartisan talks to address the issue. The hopes of a possible solution were quickly dashed as measures presented to the House Judiciary Committee resulted in partisan shouting matches, with one lawmaker committing the tone deaf act of actually loading his weapon as he joined the committee meeting via Zoom.

In his address to the nation, President Biden adopted a harsher tone, demanding a ban on assault weapons and stronger Red Flag laws aimed at keeping firearms out of the hands of domestic abusers. Despite his tougher rhetoric, he also offered alternative solutions aimed once again getting bipartisan support.

When will you learn, Joe?

And it's not just Republicans who are out to stymie the Biden agenda. Big business certainly has an interest in seeing Joe fail. After the lean years of the pandemic, big business is experiencing huge profits as they drive the inflation rate to a 40 year high. Corporate CEOs have made no secret that they prefer the pro-business environment favored by Republicans. Government regulations and unions cut into their profits. So, they would certainly benefit from a change in leadership.

It's entirely possible that supply chain issues and even the baby formula shortage are efforts at sabotaging the Biden administration?

As the midterms approach, President Biden has precious little time to right the ship. Otherwise, he will face an even more hostile Republican Congress that will do everything in its power to promote a right-wing ruler... even if it's Donald Trump.

◆◆◆

Biden Responsible for Energy Inflation? "Rubbish"

By Bob Gatty

December 26, 2022

During the recent election campaign, Inflation, including the high price of gasoline, was one of the huge issues on which Republicans focused as they fought to overtake Congress.

"Rubbish," says energy expert and author Jack L. Kerfoot, when asked on the Lean to the Left podcast if it was legitimate to blame increasing prices on President Biden.

"I think it's important to realize that inflation is not a US issue," Kerfoot says in the podcast interview, now streaming. "When people talk about, it's because of the president, my comment response is rubbish," he declares.

Kerfoot pointed out that the US produces about 1.1 million barrels of oil a day, more than any other country in the world, but that we consume about 1.8 million barrels a day. "So, when we have Covid, demand drops, when we have higher gas prices, demand drops as well. But we have to realize, if we look at inflation from January of this year through November of this year, inflation in the US is about 7.1% compared to 12% in Russia and Italy, 11% in the United Kingdom, 10% in Germany, 7.3% in Australia, 7% in Canada, and 4% in Japan," he explains.

"So, what we're seeing is inflation is a global issue for multiple reasons. The real issue with oil and gas right now, or fossil fuels is the volatility because we are seeing the demand surge. When people think the demand for oil is gonna go up, the price goes up, and when it doesn't, then it, drops as well.

"A year and a half ago, just to show the impact of supply and demand, oil producers in Texas were trying to sell oil to the refineries in the Houston area, but they actually had to pay the refiners $30 a barrel to take the oil. And the reason for that is the storage tanks were completely full," he says.

"And the refiners, the only way they could take the oil is to rent cargo ships, and they had to pay a significant price for that. So, we've actually seen oil drop as low as minus $30, and we've seen it jump as high as almost 150, $160 a barrel. It's a commodity, and so we're going to see that yo-yo back and forth.

"For businesses, when you're trying to plan your business and you're trying to figure out what your heating costs are going to be, or fuel costs are going to be, how do you forecast that? Sure. So, you tend to put in a little bit of additional extra cost in there, anticipating the volatility. That uncertainty contributes to it as well.

Kerfoot points out that another factor in play is Covid in China, the largest manufacturer of goods around the world. Because of their Covid policy, in the major port city of Shanghai with over 30 million people, "when they had over a few hundred cases of Covid, they locked down the entire city. All the businesses were closed, all the apartments were locked in. People couldn't go out and unless they had special passes to the grocery store, everything was locked down."

"They've been doing that for years, which is why when we read about the shortage of the Apple phones, particularly the Apple iPhones that were being made in China, all of a sudden there was all this concern because the whole plant was shut down because of outbreaks of Covid," Kerfoot explains. "Additionally, now they've now gone the other 180 degrees in the other direction and basically said Covid is not no longer a problem. We're not worried about it" despite somewhere around 40 to 50 million cases of Covid today.

"So that's disrupting the supply chain, and then of course, if we look at the industrialized countries, let's start with the US. When our economy was coming out of covid, businesses were looking to rehire and to staff back up. And the desire for people to come back into the workforce. They were tentative, which is understandable. And as a result, they were having to pay bonuses and increase salaries to entice people back. And that was passed on to the people as well. So, if you actually look at our inflation rates, that we have in the US, more than half of that was increased wages to workers because of the necessity of a supply shortage, the worker coming back to the businesses.

"So, can President Biden impact any of that? Of course not," Kerfoot declares. "He can't, nor can any president, whether he's red or blue. From that standpoint. So, I, it causes me concern when I hear that because we're not talking about facts and not, we're not looking at the real issues at hand. We're just trying to throw mud at somebody because we don't like of their political persuasion."

◆◆◆

Who Will Best Preserve Our Democracy? Biden or Trump?

By Bob Gatty

June 26, 2024

It was shocking to read in The Washington Post that while many voters say preserving our democracy is a critical issue, a majority of swing state voters polled in a recent survey say they trust Donald Trump, not Joe Biden, to protect us from those threats.

The poll, conducted by The Washington Post and the Schar School of Policy and Government at George Mason University, revealed that more than half the voters questioned In six swing states won narrowly by Biden in 2020, said they trust the convicted felon Trump more than Biden on that issue.

That is remarkable since it is Trump, not Biden, who said he will be "a dictator" on his first day in office. It is Trump, not Biden, who has refused to accept the results of the 2020 election, which he falsely claims was rigged. It is Trump, not Biden, who engineered the January 6, 2021 insurrectionist attack on the U.S. Capitol, as he tried to coerce then Vice President Mike Pence to overthrow the election results. It is Trump, not Biden, who has played kissy-face with Putin and other dictators, not Biden.

Who Will Best Preserve Our Democracy?

The Post said that among key-state voters who identify as locked-in Biden supporters, 78 percent see threats to democracy as extremely important, while that's true of 71 percent of Trump loyalists. Threats to democracy are second only to the economy in the percentage of swing state voters overall who describe the issue as extremely important.

According to The Post, more than 7 in 10 believe Trump will not accept the results of the election if he loses, compared with one-third who say the same for Biden. Nearly half, 47 percent, say Trump would try to rule as a dictator if he is elected to another term as president, compared with 15 percent who say Biden would do that.

All of that is scary enough except that if Trump should win the election, he is likely to have a vice president who shares his same values and beliefs. And since he is 78 years of ag, it is not inconceivable that VP could end up succeeding Trump in the White House, which is why so many of those politicians want the job.

So, What About the Vice President?

Potential running mates for Trump refuse to commit to accepting the November election results, regardless of who wins, as recent media interviews highlighted by the Democratic National Committee (DNC) have revealed.

In fact, the DNC noted, "Election denialism is a litmus test in Trump's MAGA veepstakes, and VP contenders are bending over backwards to push his lies and refuse to commit to accepting this November's election results."

Said DNC Rapid Response Director Alex Floyd, "For every one of convicted felon Donald Trump's VP contenders, our democracy and the rule of law takes a backseat to Trump and his MAGA extremism. Here's what they are defending: Trump's baseless election denialism, plans to be a dictator on 'day one', and promises to pardon the insurrectionists he rallied to attack the Capitol on January 6. All of Trump's potential running mates are willing to whitewash Trump's anti-democratic extremism just to chase a spot on his ticket, but the American people won't stand for it."

The DNC today posted this summary of potential Trump VP picks and their responses when asked if they would accept the 2024 election results:

NBC News: "**Burgum**, like other contenders, has declined to comment on whether he would accept the 2024 election results."

HuffPost: "**[J.D. Vance]** said he would accept a Biden win only if he considered the election to be legitimate."

Washington Post: "Senator **Marco Rubio** of Florida, who has been floated as a possible running mate for former President Donald J. Trump, on Sunday refused to commit to accepting the results of the 2024 presidential election and repeated conspiracy theories about the 2020 election."

Washington Post: "Sen. **Tim Scott** (R-S.C.) was pressed at least six times in a TV interview Sunday on whether he would accept this November's results. He repeatedly declined to do so... He continued to evade the question even as the interviewer, NBC News's Kristen Welker, reminded him that a 'hallmark of our democracy is that both candidates agree to a peaceful transfer of power.'"

NBC News: "In an appearance on NBC News' 'Meet the Press' in January, **Stefanik** declined to commit to accepting the 2024 election results."

Laura Coates, CNN: "Will you accept the results of the 2024 election regardless of who wins, yes or no?"

Ben Carson: "I will accept the results if it's done in a fair and transparent way... let me put it this way: In the 2020 election, there were a lot of irregularities."

Abby Phillip, CNN: "If Donald Trump loses the election in 2024, will you accept the results of that election?"

Byron Donalds: "My answer has been very clear on this. "Phillip: "It's a yes or no question. Donalds: *refuses to commit to accepting the results.* Phillip: "So your answer is conditional on– based on?" Donalds: "My answer is always conditional."

Daily Beast: "Sen. **Tom Cotton** Says He'll Accept 2024 Election Results—With a Condition"

Josh Meny, 2 News Nevada: "Do you have any regrets about picking Mike Pence as your vice president? And what will you do differently this time around when you're vetting your VP?" Trump: "Mike did a good job until the end when he didn't have the courage to do what you have to do. … if he did that, I believe you would have had different election results."

NBC News: "None of these potential vice-presidential picks have committed to accepting the 2024 election results, whether Trump wins or loses."

Washington Post: "Top Republicans, led by Trump, refuse to commit to accept 2024 election results". "The question has become something of a litmus test, particularly among the long list of possible running mates for Trump. … The GOP's desire to appease Trump's fixation on 2020 now appears to loom over his search for a running mate."

MSNBC: "Potential GOP running mates hedge on accepting election results"

Axios: "Trump and his allies will want a VP pick that is more willing to comply with the former president's wishes, which former Vice President Pence rejected by certifying the 2020 results."

No wonder voters are confused about who to trust when it comes to preserving and protecting our democracy. Trump and his butt-kissing suppli-cants who want to be his VP keep filling the airwaves and social media with lies and propaganda, which all too many people believe.

Who will best preserve our Democracy? Biden or Trump? What do you think?

◆◆◆

Should Biden be Replaced? A Conversation About Attracting Young Voters

By Bob Gatty

June 30, 2024

Former presidential candidate Jason Palmer, who challenged President Biden for the Democratic nomination, is urging Democrats to replace Biden with a younger candidate who would attract the support of young voters and independents.

It's a position that Palmer held as he sought the nomination himself, not one that resulted only from Biden's poor performance in his June 27 debate with Donald Trump. But now that he's dropped out of the race, Palmer has launched a new organization called Together!, aimed at reducing political polarization and empowering young voters to foster bipartisan leadership.

On this month's Dixie Dems episode of the Lean to the Left podcast, Palmer, an accomplished venture capitalist and an influential leader in the technology and innovation sectors, discusses his groundbreaking initiative. He joins Dixie Dems regular panelists, Arthur Hill from North Carolina and Robert Thompson from Georgia, and myself representing South Carolina, as we share our insights on key political developments.

Should Biden be Replaced?

"Honestly, it pained my heart to watch that debate," Palmer recalls. "I really went into the debate hoping that President Biden and President Trump would both set kind of a positive vision for the future. That's really important to me and make people feel great about the potential leadership for the country.

"And I saw one man up there who was lying all the time in every single answer and just demonstrating no character. And then I saw President Biden up there saying a lot of things that if you looked at the transcript, he was saying correct, factual information, but the most important thing he needed to show was energy and that he could be a fighter on behalf of the American people and that you could beat Trump. And honestly, he fell short on that."

"I want Democrats to have a very thoughtful and in public conversation about the fact that there are better candidates to run against Trump this fall, who not only have a better chance of winning, but who actually have a positive vision for the future," Palmer says.

"We should thank him and honor him for his 50 years of service. But it's time for him to be like George Washington and say, it's time for me to pass that torch to the next generation."

His answer to the question "Should Biden be Replaced?" was clear. The Democrats, he says, should have a serious conversation about how to do that.

The Mission of Together!

Palmer's vision for Together! is to engage and mobilize a million young voters in battleground states this fall. The initiative will endorse 20 young, technologically savvy candidates committed to bipartisanship. These candidates need to sign a pledge to join the Problem Solvers Caucus in the House of Representatives once elected and work towards constructive bipartisan solutions. Currently, Together! has publicly endorsed four candidates: Frank Pierce in North Carolina, Rebecca Cook in Wisconsin, Louisa Kuaea in American Samoa, and Adam Frisch in Colorado.

Palmer stressed the strategic importance of these candidacies, highlighting how they are poised to infuse fresh perspectives into Congress. He expects the roster of Together! -endorsed candidates -- nine Democrats, nine Republicans, and two independents, to be completed over the summer, perhaps by the end of July.

Palmer emphasizes the critical need for funds to support Together!'s ambitious agenda. Although the initiative is equipped to operate with half a million dollars, the goal is to raise $20 million. Contributions are being sought from individuals, PACs, and corporations, with various fundraising mechanisms including a Kickstarter campaign that involves college sports stars and others. To learn more, please visit https://TogetherPurple.org.

Regional Political Updates

In a segment discussing regional political updates, Arthur Hill and Robert Thompson bring to light key issues in North Carolina and Georgia. Hill discusses the intense gubernatorial race in North Carolina and the legislature's controversial changes to campaign finance laws. Thompson talks about the dangerous climate for election workers in Georgia and key electoral races, emphasizing the critical need for competent and fair representation.

❖❖❖

Mr. President, Please Pass the Torch

By Bob Gatty

July 8, 2024

Following President Biden's recent interview with ABC, Rep. James Clyburn, the South Carolina Democrat who helped him secure the nomination four years ago, said "Biden is who our country needs."

He made similar comments back when Biden first ran against Donald Trump, and he was correct. Joe Biden then was exactly who our country needed following the disastrous four years of Trump's presidency. His performance as our president has proved the accuracy of those words, and we all should be grateful for what this kind, caring man has done for our country.

When Biden and Vice President Kamala Harris took office four years ago, America faced a ranging pandemic, an economic crisis, a climate crisis, and racial injustice. They promised to move quickly to tackle these issues and that's exactly what they have done. And yes, there is more to do.

Biden Accomplishments

Just last week, the Bureau of Labor Statistics reported that total non-farm payroll employment increased by 206,000 in June, with the unemployment rate at 4.1 percent. While Republicans blame Biden for high inflation, it is steadily coming down. Now, the Federal Planning Bureau forecasts that average consumer price inflation should be 3.2 percent by years end and just 2.0 percent in 2025, compared to 4.06 percent last year and 9.59 percent in 2022 -- a rate largely attributable to the pandemic, which Trump thoroughly mismanaged.

Under the Biden administration, the Inflation Reduction Act helped lower costs for families, reducing the deficit and making the largest corporations pay their fair share.

Tackling the high cost of prescription drugs, that new law allows Medicare to negotiate the price of certain high-cost drugs, for example capping the cost of a month's supply of insulin at $35. Moreover, related actions by Biden have caused gas prices to drop by more than $1.60 per gallon from their peak in the summer of 2022.

The list of his achievements goes on, including:

- The Bipartisan Safer Communities Act, which helps remove firearms from dangerous individuals, narrows the "boyfriend loophole," expands mental health services in schools and supports school safety.

- Rebuilding our infrastructure through the Bipartisan Infrastructure

Law.

- Protecting marriage for LGBTQ+ and interracial couples.

- Appointing Supreme Court Justice Ketanji Brown Jackson and federal judges of diverse backgrounds.

- Supporting Ukraine in response to Putin's aggression.

- Issuing executive orders protecting reproductive rights that are being threatened by Republicans.

- Doggedly working to provide student debt relief in the face of opposition by Republicans.

- Delivering an aggressive climate and environmental justice agenda.

- Providing affordable health insurance to more people than ever before.

- Helping to reduce household energy costs.

There is much more, of course, even as Biden has had to deal with the tragedy that's taking place in Gaza and its attendant domestic repercussions along with immigration and its related issues -- all while coping with stubborn opposition from Republicans and constant criticism and challenges by Trump and his MAGA supporters.

The Ravages of Age

But now, perhaps, comes his biggest test. Concerns and criticism about his age and mental fitness that have plagued Biden throughout his presidency have boiled over following his poor performance in the Trump debate, and his efforts to quell those concerns have proved to be less than effective.

Based on that debate and his subsequent performances in interviews and meetings, including one with Democratic governors at the White House, it is painfully clear that today's President Biden is a far cry from the candidate who we elected over Trump four years ago.

At 81, it is obvious that the years have taken their toll. His memory is suffering, and he often seems lost without a teleprompter. Asked during an ABC interview if he had watched his own debate performance afterwards, Biden said he wasn't sure. What? How could you not know that? While seemingly fit enough, especially when compared to the obviously overweight Trump, his movements are slow and unsteady. Tragically, none of this will go away. We simply do not get younger and stronger and more mentally fit as we age. That just does not happen.

Watching this play out is sad, indeed, and Joe Biden doesn't deserve this. However, at some point in our lives we all experience the ravages of old age -- unless we don't make it that far, of course. Nevertheless, he is the President, and as long as he holds that job, Joe Biden must deal with the vast responsibilities of the presidency.

Thus, the thought of what could happen over the next four years is one of legitimate concern. What if Putin or some other nasty dictator whom Trump emulates decides to test Biden further? How would he respond? What would he do? Fortunately, he has a Cabinet and staff to turn to for help. But then, when it's all done, he must call the shots.

Dementia is not a friend. It does not get better -- in fact, it only progresses and gets worse. Can we entrust the future and safety of our country to a President in that situation, no matter what they've done in the past, no matter how well-meaning, likeable and honest they are?

Pass the Torch

Joe Biden is a stubborn man. He obviously is angry that some fellow

171

Democrats are calling for him to "pass the torch" to a younger candidate, apparently beginning to coalesce around Vice President Harris. One of his primary election opponents even launched a petition urging him to step aside. Biden also despises Trump, says he's a danger to Democracy, and believes he is the best person to send him into permanent political retirement.

Joe Biden deserves our admiration, respect and appreciation for all that he's done in his long and laudable public service career in Congress, as Vice President, and as our President. But it is clear that he is in denial -- refusing to accept that like so many people his age, he is suffering from the ravages of time.

Some critics contend Biden's refusal to step aside is selfish. That's not the case. It simply comes from the dementia that has taken over. But, for the good of the nation, Biden needs to accept what is happening to him and step aside. That's how he can save America from Donald Trump.

Mr. President, please pass the torch. There is simply too much at stake, including our very democracy.

◆◆◆

President Biden Made the Right Call

By Bob Gatty

July 21, 2024

It was obviously an extremely difficult decision for President Biden to make, deciding to stand down and endorse Vice President Kamala Harris to succeed him as America's 47th President. But, under the circumstances, Biden made the right call.

In his letter to the American people, Biden said that "it is in the best interest of my party and the country for me to stand down and to focus solely

teleprompter," scoffed Arthur Hill.

The Dixie Dems continued to dissect Republican strategies, discussing conspiracy theories floated by Trump's supporters to garner sympathy. The conversation naturally moved to the Republican convention's unimpressive turnout and the lack of enthusiasm compared to the "historic" atmosphere surrounding Harris's candidacy.

Gun Control Talk: A Side Note

Gun control also made an appearance in the discussion. Robert Thompson expressed frustration over the continued sale of AR-15s:

"Why are we still allowing the sale and possession of AR-15s? These weapons are designed to kill, and they have no business in civilian hands."

Arthur echoed this sentiment, emphasizing that such weapons only escalate the gun violence problem in the country.

Project 2025 and Its Implications

The discussion shifted towards Project 2025, a Republican initiative aiming to revert to 1950s societal norms. Bob highlighted the dangers this project poses:

"Project 2025 aims to dismantle various federal departments, deregulate environmental protections, and divert public funds to private education institutions. It's a move back to the oil baron days."

Arthur contributed, suggesting the importance of continuing to expose and encouraged people to check out the current series on this site, explaining Project 2025's implications.

Kamala's Vice-Presidential Pick

The conversation then turned towards Harris's potential VP pick. Arthur Hill rooted for Roy Cooper, the term-limited Governor of North Carolina, highlighting his negotiation skills and appeal as a southeastern moderate.

Bob mentioned other strong contenders like Pennsylvania Governor Josh Shapiro and Arizona Senator Mark Kelly, but concerns about the latter's Senate seat led to a consensus that keeping Kelly in the Senate would be more prudent.

Social Issues and Healthcare

Towards the end, Robert brought up Georgia's lackluster transportation infrastructure and recent electricity rate hikes, contrasting with environmental moves in South Carolina where Bob recently installed solar panels.

The discussion also touched on syphilis and chlamydia rates in the Carolinas, indirectly tying the conversation back to Republicans' stances on contraception and reproductive health.

Trump's Legal Woes

The episode rounded out with some lighter, albeit no less pointed, discussion about Trump's legal battles and speculations about his future.

Arthur and Robert humorously weighed in on whether Trump would ever see jail time, with Arthur predicting that he might end up with an ankle bracelet instead. Robert said Trump probably would want it to be red, white and blue, but Bob said Trump would insist that it be branded with his name.

Kamala Harris Ignites the Democratic Party

As the episode wound down, the consensus was clear: the upcoming election is poised to be a historic one with high stakes for both sides. The team signed off with light-hearted banter and a call to stay engaged and informed in these politically charged times.

Noting that Democrats and the Harris campaign have set fundraising records since Biden's announcement, it was clear that she truly has ignited the Democratic Party -- and that Trump and the Republicans are *so* screwed.

◆◆◆

The Next Sarah Palin & Other News

By C J Waldron

August 4, 2024

When John McCain chose Sarah Palin to be his running mate in 2008, it marked the downfall of what was otherwise a well-organized campaign for the presidency and led to America electing the first Black president, Barack Obama. Is Donald Trump's choice of J.D Vance akin to anointing him the next Sarah Palin, and will it yield similar results?

Only time, and the voters, will tell.

The Next Sarah Palin

Those running for president typically choose a running mate from a competitive state to balance the ticket, so political pundits were shocked when Trump chose J.D. Vance, who is from the Republican stronghold of Ohio. Many had hoped Trump would select a running mate from one of the swing states, such as Pennsylvania or Wisconsin.

Perhaps Trump was still stinging from the "disloyal" act of his own Vice President, Mike Pence, for failing to overturn the 2020 election results. Or perhaps it might just be Trump being Trump. With his massive ego, he may have assumed that his choice didn't matter so long as he selected someone who demonstrated absolute loyalty.

Like John McCain, who Trump has openly mocked on numerous occasions, Trump may be experiencing "buyer's remorse" as Vance continues to shoot the campaign in its political foot with his verbal gaffes as past comments are unearthed that are damaging, embarrassing and downright bizarre!

Vance wasn't always on board the Trump Train. In fact, he referred to Trump as a "moral disaster" and "America's Hitler". That's not exactly the type of glowing endorsement you would expect from someone chosen to be your second in command.

With Joe Biden stepping aside, the Trump campaign switched its target to presumptive Democratic nominee, Vice President Kamala Harris. Or at least they tried to. Their pivot was a scattershot approach, where they tried throwing everything at the wall in hopes that something would stick in their attacks on Harris.

She's too soft on crime. She's too hard on criminals. She's an Ultra Liberal. Well, considering how far right the Trump campaign is, even a political centrist would be considered far left.

Never known for their originality, Trump supporters even tried resurrecting the birther controversy they used to taunt President Obama with during his time in office by claiming Harris was ineligible to run because neither of her parents were born in this country.

Apparently, the Constitutional requirements aren't part of the MAGA Constitution because Harris checks all the boxes for being able to hold the highest office in the land.

The U.S. Constitution states that the president must:

- Be a natural-born citizen of the United States

- Be at least 35 years old

- Have been a resident of the United States for 14 years

- And then J. D. Vance punched his ticket to board the crazy...er..Trump train. In one bizarre rant, he claimed he would be called a racist for drinking *Diet Mountain Dew*. He continued with his unexplainable defense of the ubiquitous soft drink, which some have called "the symbol of White hope and despair". He then went on to mock Kamala Harris's laugh while emitting his own weird cackle.

Many referred to the comments, and Vance's own awkward laughing at his own jokes as "cringe".

(Editor's Note: It was damned weird, too.)

Trump's support among suburban women has never been his strong point. He was forced to soften his stance on abortion, much to the chagrin of his White Christian base, to try to woo their votes, but stuck to outdated talking points that indicated they should take the "stand by your man" approach when selecting a president.

J.D Vance threw fuel on this proverbial fire when a 2021 interview with Fox News was discovered and shared by 2016 Presidential candidate Hillary Clinton. In the interview, Vance attacks Harris, Alexandria Ocasio-Cortez and even Transportation Secretary Pete Buttigieg for not having biological children.

In the interview he states:

"We are effectively run in this country via the Democrats, via our corporate oligarchs, by a bunch of childless cat ladies who are miserable at their own lives and the choices that they've made and so they want to make the rest of the country miserable too."

Needless to say, the "childless cat ladies" comment did not go over well, especially coming from the party that wants to ban in vitro fertilization, a method thousands of women have used to have children of their own.

So, keep up the good work, J.D.! I'm sure there will be a spot for you somewhere. Perhaps you can come up with your own brand of soft drink or even a new kind of pillow. Vance, who was once seen as the heir apparent to the MAGA dynasty, may just be the next Sarah Palin.

Vance and Project 2025

Before we leave J.D. to go off to whatever private Hell awaits him at Mar a Lago, it should be noted that he has a rather unique connection to *Project 2025,* which has been called a blueprint to Trump's second administration, should it occur. While the Trump campaign has tried to distance themselves from the Draconian proposals contained in the 900+ page right wing manifesto, Vance has embraced it, or at least he has done so with its primary author, Kevin Roberts, President of the Heritage Foundation.

You see, Roberts also has a book coming out. And the forward to this dark vision of America: *Dawn's Early Light: Taking Back Washington to Save America,* is written by none other than Vance himself. In it, Vance reflects the violent rhetoric embraced by several Republicans who suggest a Civil War would erupt if Trump loses the 2024 election.

In writing the foreword Vance states: "We are now all realizing that it's time to circle the wagons and load the muskets. In the fights that lay ahead, these ideas are an essential weapon."

The Heritage Foundation and Project 2025 are referenced in the first sentence of the book's description, which also claims "America is on the brink of destruction."

- "Chapter by chapter, it identifies institutions that conservatives need to build, others that we need to take back, and more still that are too corrupt to save: Ivy League colleges, the FBI, the *New York Times*, the National Institute of Allergy and Infectious Diseases, the Department of Education, BlackRock, the Bill and Melinda Gates Foundation, the National Endowment for Democracy, to name a few," the description reads.

- "All these need to be dissolved if the American way of life is to be passed down to future generations."

Despite this, Vance's spokesperson asserted that Vance's foreword had nothing to do with *Project 2025*.

But Vance wasn't done endorsing the lunatic fringe. He has praised the book written by Pizzagate conspiracy theorist Jack Posobiec. The book, titled *Unhumans: The Secret History of Communist Revolutions (and How to Crush Them),* describes civil rights activists and member of the Black Lives Matter movement as communists and socialists. It also calls the January 6th insurrection a hoax, while also praising those who participated in the melee as "well-meaning patriots".

While both labeling those on the left as socialists and calling the January 6th insurrection a hoax are standard MAGA talking points, labeling those on the left a "unhuman" sets a dangerous precedent. It effectively grants the right to murder Democrats because, since they aren't really humans as we know it, we aren't killing anything vital. This is reflective of the Nazi propaganda used to exterminate the Jewish population during the Holocaust and even America's own dark past when slaves were viewed not as people, but property to be used as needed. Keep those recommendations coming, J. D.! The infomercial world needs people like you!

I Won't Back Down (Until I Do)

Joe Biden's downfall came during the first of what was to be two presidential debates. His complete lack of clarity and slack-jawed appearance made him ultimately realize that, for democracy to survive, he would need to step aside.

When Kamala Harris emerged as the Democratic front-runner, Trump initially said he would be happy to debate her instead of Biden "Any time. Anywhere". But since the Olympics are currently underway, Trump has now decided he will enter himself in the Backpedaling event. At first, he complained that he had agreed to only debate Joe Biden. Then he whined about the debate sponsor, ABC, and its moderator, George Stephanopoulos. He demanded the debate be moved to his right-wing propaganda network, Fox News.

He is now claiming that he won't commit to debating Harris until a Democratic candidate is chosen. Yet, he debated Joe Biden after ducking every contest with his Republican opponents during the primaries despite Biden not yet having the official endorsement of his party.

Trump's own daughter in law, and chosen RNC chair, Lara Trump, released a song in praise of her father-in-law. In what can best be termed a drunken karaoke rendition, the younger Trump sang (?) the late Tom Petty's "I Won't Back Down" as a mantra for the elder's refusal to back away from any challenge.

Perhaps it's time to change your tune, Lara. But please, don't sing his praises anymore!

We are at a critical time in our nation's history. The lunatics are threatening to take over the asylum and murder those who disagree with them.

The time for action is NOW!

Vote Blue!

◆◆◆

The GOP's Trump Loyalty Dilemma

By Bob Gatty

August 6, 2024

Despite Donald Trump's many legal and moral abuses, most Republican party leaders continue to support him. Now, why is that? How can we explain Republican complicity?

What's happened to the GOP where unquestioning Trump loyalty is now more important than traditional conservative values?

These questions were addressed in a new episode of the Lean to the Left podcast featuring Bob Gatty and author Kristen Monroe, who provides a deep analysis of today's GOP mindset through her book *Politics, Principle, and Standing Up to Donald Trump, Moral Courage in the Republican Party*.

Monroe's book, co-authored with 13 students and published by Ethics International Press Limited in the UK, includes insightful interviews from prominent Trump critics like Anthony Scaramucci and Lincoln Project co-founder Rick Wilson.

Monroe, a professor at the University of California at Irvine, delves into the issues of courage, politics, and the Trump phenomenon. Her new analysis suggests that the GOP's unwavering support for Trump could be profoundly harmful to our democracy.

When asked what prompted her to undertake this detailed analysis, Monroe shared her journey and the contributions of her students in the research process. Monroe's personal background in studying moral courage and ethical leadership intersected perfectly with the political realities of the Trump era, pushing her and her students to explore why only a handful of Republicans stood against Trump.

Republican Leaders' Shift in Loyalty

Numerous leading Republicans who once criticized Trump, like Sen. Lindsey Graham (R-SC) and Senator J.D. Vance (R-OH), have now become his staunch supporters. Monroe suggests that their behavior might stem from political opportunism, fear of losing Trump's base, or even potential blackmail, as observed by figures like Scaramucci. It's all about the GOP's Trump loyalty dilemma.

The case of Mitch McConnell stands out as especially puzzling to Monroe. Initially, McConnell claimed that Trump's role in the January 6th insurrection was impeachable, but later ensured that the Senate did not convict Trump. Monroe finds McConnell's actions baffling, considering Trump's antagonistic behavior towards McConnell and his wife, Elaine Chao, who was Trump's Labor Secretary.

A significant point discussed was whether GOP leaders have core values. Monroe believes that those who opposed Trump, like Liz Cheney and Adam Kinzinger, acted from a place of conscience and moral courage, driven by their commitment to the oath of office and democratic principles.

Trump's Appeal to MAGA Followers

Trump's appeal to MAGA followers, including deeply religious Christians, is another perplexing phenomenon. Monroe suggests that Trump tapped into a populist, authoritarian appeal that resonated with people who felt overlooked and aggrieved by the system. His ability to create a narrative of being their savior has solidified their support, despite his personal indiscretions and lack of genuine policy proposals.

Monroe extends this discussion to explain how Trump's constant state of chaos and crisis has nurtured a dependency among his followers. This behavior is consistent with populist and authoritarian leaders throughout history, who create and exploit crises to maintain power and control.

The Transformation of the Republican Party

Monroe points out that Trump has fundamentally changed the Republican Party as traditional conservative values have been sidelined in favor of loyalty to Trump. Monroe contends that many Republicans have been driven by their core beliefs in democracy and human decency to oppose Trump, but these voices are increasingly marginalized.

Kamala Harris and Women's Rights

The conversation also touched on Vice President Kamala Harris's potential as a unifying and galvanizing figure for critical communities, especially women and young people. Monroe believes Harris's strengths lie in her ability to appeal to diverse groups, crucial for building a broad coalition.

The Importance of Voting

The overarching message of the interview was the importance of voting in preserving democracy. Monroe emphasizes that the November election is critical, asserting that the very foundations of American civic culture and democracy are at stake. She urges every citizen to participate in the electoral process to ensure that democratic ideals prevail.

A Call to Action

Kristen Monroe's analysis and insights are a call to action for all concerned about the future of American democracy. Her body of work, including *When Conscious Calls* and her latest book, underscores the importance of moral courage and ethical leadership in times of political turbulence. As the November election approaches, Monroe's plea for civic engagement and informed voting is more crucial than ever.

Additionally, for more in-depth discussions on Project 2025 and its implications, please check out our special series of articles explaining the significance of key components of this GOP manifesto.

Special Thanks

We extend our heartfelt gratitude to Professor Kristen Monroe for sharing her expertise and joining us on the Lean to the Left podcast. Her critical insights contribute significantly to the ongoing dialogue about the future of American democracy.

◆◆◆

Could Civil War Return?

By Bob Gatty

August 16, 2024

In new episode of the Lean to the Left podcast, author William R. Douglas, discusses the unsettling topic of a possible second American Civil War, a theme central to his new book, "The Sum of All Our Anger." The conversation takes listeners on a deep dive into the author's thoughts, his inspiration, and the stark realities he imagines in his dystopian future.

A Nation Divided: Could Civil War Return?

With the increasing political divisiveness in the United States, Douglas speculates about a future where these fractures lead to a catastrophic civil conflict. The storyline explores how political rhetoric, and actions could potentially escalate to violent unrest, creating a scenario where Americans might once again take up arms against each other.

Interestingly, Douglas's first steps towards writing this book were inspired by his previous work, "The Death and Resurrection of Baseball." In that novel, a civil war served as an underlying theme that intrigued readers to the extent that they encouraged Douglas to explore it further. With the political atmosphere in the country growing increasingly tense, Douglas felt compelled to delve into this frightening possibility. For our interview with Douglas about that book, please click here.

A Futuristic Dystopia

Speaking about his novel, William Douglas paints a chilling picture of a future America divided along harsh ideological lines. His narrative is set in 2060, where a new liberal president enforces socialism, alters the national flag, and sparks turmoil. Douglas chose to explore the far-left's rise to power, something he observed as having potential real-world implications given current political trends. Could civil war return? Douglas believes it's possible if things don't change.

The Secession of Texas

One pivotal moment in his novel is the secession of Texas from the United States, symbolizing a tipping point that triggers the second civil war. Douglas elaborates on the economic power of Texas and its potential to thrive independently, which adds a layer of plausibility to his fictional scenario. The secession, followed by a federal backlash, effectively sets the stage for the unfolding chaos in the narrative.

Censorship and Culture War

Douglas also touches on the contentious issue of cancel culture, magnified in his book through the banning of patriotic songs and the dismantling of cherished monuments. He explains that his depiction of such extreme measures reflects current debates around history, identity, and national symbols, projecting them into an exaggerated but conceivable future.

Despite the bleak storyline, Douglas assures readers that his intent is not to incite fear but to serve as a deterrent. His goal is for readers to reflect on the importance of dialogue, compromise, and the need to avoid extreme polarization.

Learning from The Past

Throughout the podcast, Douglas draws parallels between the fictional and real worlds, emphasizing the lessons history teaches us about division and conflict. He highlights the need for political moderation and for Americans to purge extremism from both sides of the political spectrum.

A noteworthy part of the interview was Douglas's advocacy for civil discourse. He stresses the importance of conversations among diverse groups to encourage understanding and unity. He uses examples from history, such as the bipartisan relationship between President Reagan and Speaker Tip O'Neill, to illustrate how political adversaries can work together for the national good.

Douglas hopes that "The Sum of All Our Anger" will inspire readers to critically evaluate the current trajectory of American politics and foster a spirit of cooperation and patriotism. He leaves listeners with a powerful message: even in the face of deep disagreements, it is possible to find common ground and work towards a better future.

◆◆◆

Kamala Harris, Trump, and Woke Politics

By Bob Gatty

August 19, 2024

An enlightening episode of the Lean to the Left podcast delves into critical social issues with Richard Pellegrino, author of **"I'm Not White, One Man's Journey from Whiteness to Oneness"** and founder of the Global Woke Institute. Through an eye-opening conversation, Pellegrino shares his personal experiences and insights on race, identity, politics, and what it means to be truly "woke."

Kamala Harris, Trump, and Woke Politics

The discussion opens with the significant political milestone of Vice President Kamala Harris being the Democratic nominee for president. Is America ready for a black female president?

Despite the prevalent issues of sexism and racism, especially among certain conservative segments, Pellegrino emphasizes the importance of Harris's nomination as a symbol of America's progress. He humorously points out, "Thank God a black woman's going to kick someone's butt."

Thus, the headline: Kamala Harris, Trump, and Woke Politics.

Personal Journey from Whiteness to Oneness

Pellegrino recounts his journey from being deeply embedded in a life of privilege and drug addiction to becoming an advocate for racial unity and spiritual awakening. His memoir serves not only as a legacy for his family, but also as a testament to his personal transformation influenced by notable figures like Kendi and Dr. King.

"I woke up, that's when I had my initial awakening," he says, highlighting the importance of self-awareness and continual growth.

The Role of Family and Multiracial Identity

Pellegrino's multiracial family has profoundly impacted his perspectives and work. He talks about his West Indian wife and their eight children, emphasizing the beauty and complexity of their multiracial heritage.

He humorously notes, "I'm a recovering Catholic too, Italian, but anyway, but yeah, Bob, we're actually the most... multiracial." This personal narrative underscores the interconnectedness of racial and cultural identities.

From Activism to Spiritual Awakening

Pellegrino reflects on how the activism and cultural movements of the 1970s shaped his early years. He admits that his initial understanding of racial issues was intellectual rather than heartfelt, until life experiences, including severe drug addiction and spiritual exploration, led him to a deeper comprehension.

His transformative journey involved studying various spiritual practices, ultimately leading him to the Baha'i faith, which teaches the unity of all races and religions.

Discussing the challenges Vice President Kamala Harris faces, Pellegrino suggests that her greatest obstacles might come from within the Democratic and broader progressive movements, rather than from external opposition. He stresses the importance of unity and collaboration within these groups to combat the divisiveness that can weaken their efforts.

The Global Woke Institute and Redefining "Woke"

The conversation shifts to the Global Woke Institute, where Pellegri-

191

no reveals his aim to redefine and reclaim the term "woke" to mean "oneness." He believes that true awakening involves recognizing our global interconnectedness and the impact of our actions on the world. By fostering this understanding through the Institute, he hopes to inspire individuals to live more consciously and compassionately.

Pellegrino discusses the concept of global citizenship, advocating for a shift away from narrow national identities toward a broader, humanitarian perspective. He stresses that addressing global issues like poverty, climate change, and equity is essential for achieving a more just and sustainable world. He echoes the sentiments of organizations like Global Citizen, highlighting the importance of collective action and mutual aid.

Personal Takeaways and a Call to Action

Throughout the podcast, Pellegrino's passion for social justice and his commitment to living a purposeful life shine through. He shares his belief in the power of individual actions to drive systemic change, urging listeners to awaken to their own roles in shaping a better future. As he aptly concludes, "We're all in it together."

For those inspired by Richard Pellegrino's message, the Global Woke Institute offers resources and opportunities for engagement. Visit **HowWokeAmI.org** to take the self-assessment test, explore educational materials, and find out how you can contribute to this global movement.

This episode serves as a powerful reminder of the ongoing journey toward equity, unity, and spiritual awakening. By embracing our shared humanity and working together, we can create a world that truly reflects the values of oneness and justice.

◆◆◆

Hey Trump, Does Size Matter?

By Bob Gatty

August 21, 2024

Donald Trump is obsessed with size; the size -- or lack thereof-- of his crowds, the size of the opposition's crowds, the size of his hands, and perhaps by extension, the size of his manhood, which Stormy Daniels described in some detail in her book and during court testimony that led to Trump's felony conviction in his hush money trial.

But on the second night of the Democratic National Convention in Chicago, Trump's arch enemy, former President Barack Obama and First Lady Michelle Obama, artfully stuck it to Trump, and that, my friends, must have really gotten under his skin.

it was a one-two punch from which the Orange One may never recover. And, it wasn't just the size of crowds, or whatever, there was more. Much more. Like "black jobs" and wealth, or the lack thereof. And then there were the top Republicans who spoke at the DNC against him.

Does Size Matter?

Said Obama, "It has been a constant stream of gripes and grievances that's actually been getting worse now that he's afraid of losing to Kamala. There are the childish nicknames. The crazy conspiracy theories. This weird obsession with crowd sizes."

And with that, Obama held his hands a few inches apart, bringing howls of laughter from the huge crowd inside the convention hall. He said no more about that, but delegates quickly got the point.

Obama called Trump "a guy whose act has gotten pretty stale" and said he's "a 78-year-old billionaire who hasn't stopped whining about his problems since he rode down his golden escalator nine years ago."

Obama's comments came after the former First Lady called out Trump on race.

"His limited, narrow view of the world made him feel threatened by the existence of two hard-working highly educated successful people who happened to be Black. Who's gonna tell him that the job he is currently seeking might just be one of those Black jobs," she said, once again to loud and long cheers from the assembled delegates.

And then, there was Illinois Gov. JB Pritzker who mocked Trump and reminded us of some of the stupid, ridiculous events from his presidency, including suggesting injecting bleach to potentially cure the coronavirus.

And Pritzker, an air to the Hyatt Hotel fortune and an actual billionaire, let loose with a dig about Trump's purported wealth.

"Take it from an actual billionaire," he said, "Trump is rich in only one thing, stupidity."

That was funny, and the convention delegates thought so, too.

The Republicans

But what about the Republicans -- some of them big shots -- who showed up to speak in support of Democratic presidential nominee Vice President Kamala Harris and her running mate, Minnesota Gov. Tim Walz.

Former Trump communications director and close Trump adviser Stephanie Grisham said she was an original "true believer" but that "behind closed doors Trump mocks his supporters" and calls them "basement dwellers."

"He used to tell me 'it doesn't matter what you say, Stephanie, just say it enough and people will believe you,'" she revealed.

"He has no empathy, no morals, and no fidelity to the truth," said Grisham, explaining that she declined to hold White House press briefings because of Trump's lies. "Unlike my boss, I never wanted to stand at the podium and lie," she said.

Other Republicans speaking at the DNC include Ana Navarro-Cárdenas of *The View*, host of night two of the convention, former Illinois Representative Adam Kinzinger, former Pence adviser Olivia Troye, and a three-time Trump voter working in construction, Kyle Sweetser.

"I started to see Trump's tariff policy in action, costs for construction workers like me were starting to soar," Sweetser said. "I realized Trump wasn't for me, he was for lining his own pockets."

Assuring the crowd that he's not "left-wing," Sweetser said, "I believe our leaders should bring out the best in us. Not the worst. That's why I'm voting for Kamala Harris."

Other leading Republicans speaking at the DNC are from key battleground states: John Giles, the mayor of Mesa, Arizona, and Geoff Duncan, the former lieutenant governor of Georgia.

But there are plenty of former speakers at previous Republican National Conventions who no longer support Trump, including:

- Trump's former vice president, Mike Pence, spoke at the last two RNC conventions but has refused to endorse Trump's 2024 campaign

- Former GOP presidential nominee Mitt Romney, a three-time RNC convention speaker, has said he would "absolutely not" vote for Trump.

- Former GOP vice presidential nominee Paul Ryan spoke at the RNC convention in 2012 and 2016 but will not be voting for Trump in November.

- Chris Christie spoke at the 2012 and 2016 RNC conventions, but now says he will not support Trump "under any circumstances."

- Former Ohio governor John Kasich spoke at the 2012 RNC convention, but has now repeatedly rebuked Trump and his MAGA extremism.

- Former House GOP member Barbara Comstock was the co-chair of the 2012 RNC convention and now says Trump is a "horrible misogynist."

- U.S. Ambassador to Kenya Meg Whitman spoke at the 2008 RNC convention and has since blasted Trump as a "dishonest demagogue."

So, if size matters to Trump, how does he feel about the dwindling size of his own GOP supporters? That's got to rankle him, big time.

◆◆◆

One Nutcase Joins Another

By Bob Gatty

August 25, 2024

Robert F. Kennedy, Jr., the man who had a parasitic worm in his brain, and tried to get Kamala Harris to give him a job in her new administration, has dropped out of the presidential sweepstakes and is backing another nutcase, Donald J. Trump.

They deserve each other and make a great match considering that Trump, while his brain apparently is worm-free, is about as wacko as you can get considering that during the Covid pandemic he tossed out the idea of injecting people with bleach to prevent the onset of the virus that's claimed more than 1.2 million people, mostly on his watch.

And remember what he said in 2020: "I don't take responsibility at all."

OK, so now worm-brain RFK Jr. has hooked up with Trump in his effort to derail the Harris-Walz march to the White House. It's a great fit, too, because Kennedy once sent a friend a pic of himself with what he claimed to be a barbecued dog cooked on a spit. So, he should get along great with Trump's VP running mate JD Vance, who apparently has something against cats.

A lot of women are pissed off at Vance for saying the U.S. is being run by Democrats, corporate oligarchs and "a bunch of childless cat ladies who are miserable at their own lives and the choices they've made and so they want to make the rest of the country miserable, too."

Getting Weirder by the Minute

Wow! That is weird! How does that dovetail with all the joy the Kamala Harris-Tim Walz team is bringing to the presidential campaign -- and, really, the nation? It's especially weird, too, because it's the Republicans who are being run by corporate oligarchs who Trump is trying to hit up for campaign cash, not the Democrats who are laser focused on helping the middle class.

Anyway, the Democratic National Committee"s War Room has emailed a press release with reactions to the RFK Jr's support of Trump, as he apparently has given up hopes of working in the Harris administration because Kamala refused to take his call. So, he's now switching to Trump where he must think he could find a job. Hopefully, however, it would not be as dog catcher.

Here are some of the comments published by the War Room following Kennedy's endorsement of Trump:

The Hill: GOP strategist cautions Trump on joining forces with RFK Jr: 'He's kind of a looney tune'.

"Republican strategist Scott Jennings advised former President Trump to be careful now that he has seemingly joined forces with Robert F. Kennedy Jr., arguing the independent presidential candidate is 'kind of a looney tune.' [...] 'There could be some cost on the other side of the algebra...he's a conspiracy theorist, and a lot of people think he's kind of a looney tune.'"

Stuart Stevens on MSNBC with Ali Velshi

"Well, you know, Donald Trump objects to being called weird. So, what does he do...he goes and takes this endorsement from, you know, one of the sadder figures in American public life. A guy who clearly is just broken...you have two candidates that are supporting Putin, two candidates who would like to end the war in Ukraine so that Russia could take Ukraine, and you have two candidates who are against any mandatory vaccines in schools... that's the pro—polio route. I mean, it is just as nutty as it can be, and it will continue to dismay me that other members of my former party don't call it out. It's just crazy."

Ronald Brownstein with CNN's Michael Smerconish

"And I think this latent threat to Trump of being associated with anti-vaccine extremism that Kennedy brings to him, I think on balance, this will end up being more of a problem than an asset."

Scott Jennings and Karen Finney on State of the Union with Jake Tapper

Jennings: "My caution, my advice, would be the downstream effects of this. You now own anything [RFK Jr.] might do or say for the next couple of months, and this may or may not inure your benefits. So, I would just caution, careful, careful."

Finney: "If you want to have that endorsement, I'm perfectly happy for you to because that's fine. I mean, people who take dead bear cubs to Central Park... if you want that vote, go for it."

"I think the more people know about Bobby Kennedy the more people who are sane will not want to vote for him. I think he is a perfect match for Donald Trump. And in fact, if I were JD Vance, I would stick by the phone, because he might be just the kind of guy that Trump would pull in as an October surprise. He is freakish in every sense of the word, whether it's picking up bear roadkill or eating a barbecue dog. But much more seriously, he's a nut. He is a conspiracy nut. He's a racist."

And so, indeed, worm-brain RFK, Jr. is a perfect match for Trump as one nutcase joins another. Walz got it right. Those guys really are weird.

◆ ◆ ◆

A Fact of Life

By C J Waldron

September 6, 2024

There was another school shooting, this time in rural Georgia, home of MAGA maven Majorie Taylor Greene. She touted the all- too-often heard mantra of offering prayers for the dead and wounded, but no concrete solution to the deadly epidemic of gun violence plaguing our schools.

And where was Donald Trump on the issue? In his typical rambling, incoherent, devoid of solutions response during a Fox News Town Hall, he vowed to "heal our world" in the wake of yet another mass casualty shooting. Instead of elaborating on what he would do, he trailed off and began commenting on wars and how "sick and angry" we are over the incompetence of our leaders.

So, instead of offering solutions, he allowed his running mate, JD Vance, to address the issue.

Big mistake. HUGE!!

Rather than condemn the violence, Vance did what he does best. He threw gasoline onto the fire. He said that school shootings are simply a "fact of life". Basically, he implied that kids should get used to being shot at while they are trying to get an education. He went on further to state that schools need to invest in better security rather than banning certain types of firearms.

In typical MAGA fashion, Vance wants already struggling school districts to stop wasting money on books teaching Critical Race Theory and Woke policies that are aimed at turning our children gay or grooming them to be victims of sexual abuse. Instead, he wants schools to invest in better security measures.

Vance conveniently ignored the fact that over 60 percent of Georgia schools, including the one in Winder, Georgia, have enhanced security measures. In fact, law enforcement credited these new policies as preventing an even greater loss of life.

Following the Parkland School shooting in Florida, Trump met with the survivors. In his hands, clearly visible, was a slip of paper with specific talking points that any normal human being would ask without needing prompting. After hearing them out, and following the suggestion written on the paper, Trump replied, "I hear you" and vowed to enact stricter gun control measures.

Until...

The NRA met with Trump after hearing his comments. Whatever was said in the meeting resulted in Trump's immediate backtracking on his earlier vow to the traumatized students. Instead, out of fear of losing the support of the all-powerful gun lobby, he did nothing.

Fast forward to the current campaign where Trump is telling people that he is the best friend gun owners had in the White House as he tries to curry favor with the rabid pro-Second Amendment swath of voters. He has gone on to claim that he "did nothing" to further gun restrictions. He wants them to ignore the now stricken Executive Order he issued banning bump stocks following the Las Vegas massacre.

He also wants them to forget that he almost defied the NRA by suggesting he would enact stronger gun-control measures following the Parkland shootings.

Instead, he and other MAGA Republicans want you to believe the oft-repeated lie that Democrats are "coming for your guns". It's a scare tactic they have used in multiple elections and one that MAGA followers are all too willing to accept as fact even though it has no basis in reality.

And so, children will continue to live in fear. They will continue to die needlessly. They will continue to be traumatized by lock down drills and active shooter alerts.

Oh well. It's a fact of life.

◆◆◆

Trump Can Run, but He Can't Hide

By Bob Gatty

September 13, 2024

Donald Trump, crushed by Kamala Harris in Tuesday night's debate, campaigned in Tucson, Arizona yesterday, but neither he nor his MAGA followers could hide from his disastrous debate performance.

The Democratic National Committee displayed a new mobile that circled the Tucson Music Hall throughout the day. With clips from the debate, it showed Harris calling out Trump's incoherent rants, fragile ego, and self-serving agenda.

Donald Trump, crushed by Kamala Harris in Tuesday night's debate, campaigned in Tucson, Arizona Thursday, but neither he nor his MAGA followers could hide — even though they'd like to, given his disastrous debate performance.

Now, Trump has announced that he will not participate in second debate with Harris, claiming that he won Tuesday's affair and effectively made all of his key points about immigration and the economy. However, even the bookies agreed he lost badly, and the smart money is now on Harris.

BetOnline.ag tweeted minutes before the debate that 50.9% of the money wagered on the election was on Harris while 49.1% was on Trump: https://x.com/BetOnline_ag/status/1833656308983124194

BetOnline.ag said the money has significantly shifted toward Harris, with 54.4% of the handle on the VP. We're talking about money here, folks. That's serious.

"There will be no third debate!" Trump wrote in all caps on Truth Social, "When a prizefighter loses a fight, the first words out of his mouth are, 'I want a rematch'" the former president wrote before claiming he "won the debate" based on undisclosed polls that nobody else apparently has seen.

So go ahead, Trump, run from another debate. But you can't hide. There are now 53 days until the election, plenty of time for Harris to continue exposing his lies, his attacks against women and minorities, and his foolish, bizarre behavior to the American voters.

In fact, the Democratic National Committee launched a new mobile billboard to circle the Tucson Music Hall where Trump was to speak Thursday, showing clips from the debate uplifting Harris' leadership as she calls out Trump's incoherent rants, fragile ego, and self-serving agenda.

So, no matter where they went on the streets around the Music Hall where Trump spoke, rally goers, Trump, and his entourage could not escape the billboard and its message.

Meanwhile, according to the Washington Post, Republicans are in hide mode. "Congressional Republicans try to hide from Trump's debate performance," screamed the headline.

Here's an excerpt from the story:

Speaking to reporters Wednesday, House Speaker Mike Johnson (R-La.) focused entirely on a failed government funding plan. What did he think of Trump's debate performance, reporters asked him. Johnson walked away, into the House chamber.

Across the Capitol, Sen. John Thune (R-S.D.), the No. 2 GOP leader, fell into the passive voice to avoid criticizing Trump when asked about the missed opportunity to define Vice President Kamala Harris.

"Well, um, that job's got to get done," said Thune, who is asking colleagues to promote him to majority leader.

Who should take up that task? Thune ducked into a closed luncheon for GOP senator without answering the question.

That's hardly a ringing endorsement from the two people who, if he won the presidency, Trump would rely on to advance his agenda on Capitol Hill.

So, while Thune and Johnson can run and hide from reporters' questions, Trump rally goers could not do the same as they traveled to the Music Hall in Tucson, or if they left early out of boredom with Trump and his constant whining and ridiculous claims, like immigrants from Haiti eating peoples' pets, or calling on the likes of "the late great Hannibal Lecter", as he did at a rally in Iowa.

Assassination Attempt Conspiracy Theory

During the debate, Trump said he "took a bullet to the head" in Butler, PA, probably because of Democratic rhetoric. Now, he's starting to use that scratched ear as a claim that he was shot in the head during an assassination attempt, even suggesting that somehow the Democrats were behind the shooting.

Even so, Trump apparently is making a killing from that photo of him raising his fist as red liquid ran down the side of his face. The Trump people have turned that into a fundraising initiative, selling everything from T-shirts to Christmas ornaments adorned with that fist-pump image.

There are plenty of skeptics who openly wonder if that entire event was staged by Trump and his supporters. That question is all over social media as photos of Trump shortly after event showed no evidence of any wound to the ear. So where did that red stuff come from?

We all know that Trump likes to use catsup – he tossed it against the wall in the White House one time when he was angry. Maybe there was a little left in the bottle and he used it to touch up his ear to create that photo op.

At any rate, in Tucson, Trump and his MAGA crowd were treated with reminders of his crazy debate performance as they drove around the Music Hall.

Like I said in the beginning, Trump can run, but he can't hide.

❖ ❖ ❖

Political Showdown: Trump-Harris Debate Recap

By Bob Gatty

September 16, 2024

The latest edition of the Dixie Dems on the Lean to the Left podcast features a lively discussion of the Sept. 10 Trump-Harris debate with Arthur Hill, vice-chair of the Brunswick County, NC Democratic Party and Robert Thompson, of Georgia, and host of the Got Damn Liberal podcast.

The conversation focuses on memorable moments, political implications, and personal reactions to the debate in which Trump got his butt kicked soundly by Vice President Kamala Harris, according to virtually every poll and most political experts -- including many Republicans.

There was a particularly surreal moment when Trump claimed immigrants from Haiti were stealing and eating residents' pets in Springfield, Ohio. It was an absurd comment that set the tone for a debate marked by sharp contrasts in rhetoric and demeanor between Trump and Harris.

General Reactions to the Trump-Harris Debate

Arthur Hill agreed with the initial assessment, noting that less than 24 hours after the debate, it was safe to say that "the emperor has no clothes." Hill referenced a book by Dr. Rachel Beitkofer recommending that Democrats stop moral high-grounding and start fighting back fiercely, which he felt Kamala Harris demonstrated during the debate.

Key Takeaways

1. **Immigration and Fearmongering**

   o   Hill and I were appalled by Trump's repeated, baseless comments on immigration, constantly returning to that theme throughout the debate as he reprised his claims that illegal immigrants are flooding the country, committing violent crimes, raping women, and more.

   o   Trump's claim that Haitians were eating pets in Ohio was just an example of his patently false claims.

2. **Harris's Poise and Composure**

   o   Throughout the debate, Harris presented herself as confident and composed. She handled Trump's baseless claims with remarkable equanimity. Hill commended her for standing firm against Trump, even when he resorted to juvenile name-calling and blatant misinformation.

3. **Presidential Conduct**

   o   The discussion emphasized the disparity in presidential conduct between Trump and Harris as Trump was sour, negative, and scowling, while Harris was friendly, happy, and positive.

Analyses of Specific Issues

- **Climate Change**

   o   Harris pointed out that Trump has called climate change a hoax and that while he claims to support solar energy, he still pushes the use of fossil fuels like coal and oil. Harris's position that climate change is a crucial issue for America's youth was reiterated, emphasizing the importance of a scientifically grounded approach to environmental policies.

- **Economy and Jobs**

   o   Harris deftly refuted Trump's assertions that Harris will ban fracking, a coal mining process used in Pennsylvania. She said that charge is untrue, despite her previous support for restrictions on fracking, which is harmful to the environment.

   o   Thompson pointed out that the economy is vastly improved, that inflation is declining, and that the stock market is an all-time high, refuting Trump's claims that the Biden-Harris administration is responsible for a virtual economic disaster

- **National Security and Foreign Policy**

  - Hill highlighted Harris's strong stance on Ukraine and NATO, commending her for making it clear that Trump's leniency towards Putin and Russia was detrimental to US interests. She scored points by noting the importance of NATO in curbing Russian aggression, an issue Trump seemed to misunderstand or downplay.

- **The Polls**

  - Thompson warned that even though polls are trending in favor of Harris, that the election "is not over" and Democrats need to work hard on behalf of Harris and to turn out the vote. He also noted that some analysts contend that MAGA Republicans do not respond to pollsters' calls as frequently as do liberal voters, a trend that he implied could skew the poll results in favor of Harris.

- **The Insurrection**

  - Asked if there was anything he regretted about his actions on January 6, 2021, when the mob he incited attacked the U.S. Capitol, trying to overturn the election of Joe Biden, Trump said he told his followers to go to the Capitol "peacefully."

  - Harris said she was at the Capitol that day and that Trump, then still the president, invited a violent mob to attack the Capitol, an act for which he was indicted and impeached by the House of representatives.

Conclusion

The Lean to the Left podcast's analysis of the Harris and Trump debate presents a vivid picture of a contest between positivity and negativity, truth and misinformation.

Kamala Harris, with her preparedness and poise, was seen as a leader capable of guiding the United States towards a better future. As the election approaches, the podcast underscores the critical importance of staying informed and engaged in the political process.

◆◆◆

Trump on the Defense: Harris Gains Momentum

By Bob Gatty

September 20, 2024

If the election were today, Vice President Kamala Harris would defeat former President Donald Trump by about five points, according to Doug Kaplan, president of the national polling and political consulting firm, Kaplan Strategies.

"If the election were today, Harris would win," said Kaplan, on the Lean to the Left podcast, recorded following the September 10 presidential debate, "However, two months is a long time in politics."

When asked about the enduring impact of the debate performances, Doug Kaplan said that without more debates, this singular encounter may dominate the narrative and that Harris's significant fundraising, and the Republicans' chaotic strategy underscore a potential advantage for the vice-president.

Kaplan cautioned that Harris needs to win nationally by four to five points and win the swing states by at least two points if she is to secure the election.

"Each day the election focuses on Trump is a win for Harris," said Kaplan. "Trump needs to make it about her, but he has struggled." Trumps on the defense, he added.

Kaplan pointed out Trump's vulnerability on the issue of reproductive rights, saying, "if reproductive rights inspire a high voter turnout among women, it could be a decisive factor."

Young voters could also help turn the tide for Harris, noted Kaplan, who pointed out that Barack Obama was able to capture strong support from those voters, and the question now is whether Harris can do the same.

Both immigration and the economy also will continue to be major factors, added Kaplan, as they continue to evolve.

◆◆◆

Trump's Plans for the Future? See Project 2025

By Bob Gatty
September 20, 2024

During his debate with Kamala Harris, when Donald Trump was challenged to say if he would repeal the Affordable Care Act, he claimed to have "concepts of a plan" that would result in a much better and less expensive approach to health care than the ACA.

As the Democratic National Committee said in its latest War Room dispatch, it was "the latest of Trump's cop-outs, lies, and deflections in an attempt to distract the American people from the dark reality of his second term agenda."

Trump has been trying for years to kill the ACA, always claiming that he would bring improvements that would result in better and less expensive health care. In April, he declared in a video posted to Truth Social:

"I'm not running to terminate the ACA as crooked Joe Biden says all over the place. We're going to make the ACA much better than it is right now and much less expensive for you."

Those are almost the same words he used during the debate with Harris, but after serving as president for four years, no such plan ever emerged, and the ACA is now relied upon by millions of Americans for their health care coverage.

It's in Project 2025

President Biden, and now Vice President Harris, have contended that Trump simply wants to rip away the ACA's coverage and instead make changes that would benefit private insurers and the health care industry, while eliminating coverage for pre-existing conditions.

It's just another Trump-GOP scam, and their plans can simply be found in the Heritage Foundation's Project 2025, a playbook that Republicans are pushing for the future on many fronts.

For more info on Project 2025's impact on the American people, please see our series of articles and specifically, the blog focused on health care.

As the DNC pointed out, "Trump's Project 2025 agenda would accelerate efforts to privatize Medicare and raise prescription drug prices including by getting rid of the $35/month insulin price cap for seniors established thanks to President Biden and Vice President Harris' historic Inflation Reduction Act."

In its War Room dispatch, the DNC also made these points about Trump's "plans":

Reproductive Health

Trump's only "concepts of a plan" on reproductive health care are his

Project 2025 plans to ban abortion nationwide, threaten access to IVF and contraception, and even monitor women's pregnancies.

Question: "Would you veto a national abortion ban?"[...]Trump: "Look, we don't have to discuss it."

"Republicans will, unequivocally seek to ban all abortion and make abortion inaccessible nationwide; in addition to attempting to misuse the antiquated Comstock Act to ban medication abortion, a second Trump administration could attempt to misuse the dormant statute to criminalize materials used to provide basic abortion care," said the Office of U.S. Senator Patty Murray (D-WA) regarding Project 2025.

"And by declaring that life begins at conception, his [Project 2025] manifesto appears to commit HHS to finding ways to outlaw IVF, which relies on generating multiple embryos, most of which are not implanted. The extensive mandate calls to gut reproductive freedom, including effectively banning medication abortion, ending access to emergency abortion care, attacking contraception, deploying fetal personhood, and undermining IVF in federal policy...Project 2025 would also give Trump unprecedented power to monitor pregnancies."

The Economy

Trump's only "concepts of plan" on the economy is his Project 2025 agenda to line the pockets of his billionaire buddies with tax giveaways at the expense of middle-class families.

Trump, in response to his plans for the economy: "Everybody knows what I'm going to do. Cut taxes."

Said Harris: "Donald Trump has no plan for you. And when you look at his economic plan, it's all about tax breaks for the richest people."

Trump's Project 2025 tax plan would increase taxes on the middle class while giving handouts to greedy corporations and America's wealthiest.

Border Security

Trump can't defend his actions to tank bipartisan border security legislation for his own political gain.

When he was asked why he killed the bill that would have put thousands of additional agents and officers on the border, Trump talked about the size of crowds at his rallies.

Said the DNC, "The Trump-Vance ticket will continue to prioritize political gains over policy priorities like he did when he killed the bipartisan border deal. They will work to instead implement a cruel agenda to round up people into detention camps and use the military to carry out mass deportations."

◆◆◆

Epilogue

As this is written in mid-September, it's just over one month to Election Day when America will decide whether to return to the dark days of a Donald Trump presidency or embrace the joyful, hopeful, competent presidency of Vice President Kamala Harris.

Literally our democracy is at stake.

Trump, convicted of 34 counts stemming from a scheme to illegally influence the 2016 election through a hush money payment to a porn actor, will be sentenced on November 26 unless there are further delays.

Meanwhile, Trump has been indicted in three additional criminal cases stemming from his effort to overturn the 2020 election and other actions. They include indictments in a Georgia case where he's charged with trying to overturn his loss in that state; election subversion charges brought by special council Jack Smith stemming from the January 6, 2021, insurrection at the U.S. Capitol; and charges that he illegally took classified documents from the White House to his Mar-a-Lago estate in Florida. That case, eventually dismissed by a Trump-appointed judge, but appealed by Smith, is expected to eventually be decided by the U.S. Supreme Court, which Trump has stacked with his conservative appointees.

In July the Supreme Court ruled that Trump is at least presumptively immune from criminal liability for official acts, so in early October Smith filed a new detailed brief, containing detailed information about Trump's action during the January 6 insurrection, arguing that his efforts to overturn the election were done as a candidate, not official acts as President.

The eventual outcome of these cases could mean serious penalties

213

for Trump. However, should he win the election, it is conceivable that he could end all but the Georgia case simply by pardoning himself.

So, it is possible that we could have a convicted felon – someone who would not even be eligible to vote – as the President of the United States.

But that's not all.

Trump's rhetoric has revealed his penchant for autocracy and his desire to assume the role of dictator. At one point he told supporters that this election could be their last, if only they will vote for him. He has demonstrated no understanding of or support for the U. S. Constitution and our democracy.

Harris, who ascended to the Democratic nomination after President Biden stepped aside, is the opposite of Donald Trump. Instead of warning of impending doom for America, she's offered hope while pledging to help raise the standard of living for all Americans and to require the wealthy and big business to pay their fair share in taxes.

While Trump supports governmental intrusion into the personal lives of our citizens, especially women, Harris will fight to restore Roe v. Wade, which Trump boasts of killing through his Supreme Court appointments. She supports efforts to combat climate change, which Trump calls a hoax. She opposes Trump's cruel policies on immigration and supports efforts to humanely manage the crisis at the border.

Those are just a few of the major differences for voters to consider. Hopefully, the preceding pages, which provide a virtual play-by-play of key actions by Trump and Congress, will help put into context the magnitude of what is at stake.

Above all, vote. Remember, Your vote is your voice. It's how each of us can save our nation from the darkness and cruelty of Donald J. Trump.

Afterword

The preceding pages offer a virtual play-by-play of the tragedy of the Trump presidency and the years following his defeat by President Joe Biden. Volumes 1 and 2 of *Hijacked Nation* picked up the story beginning in September 2017 running through 2020. This sequel continues the story from then until October 2024.

These past years have been a time of historic discord in America, marked by Trump's failures, marked by his determination to use the Presidency to support his wealthy friends, his donors, and to hijack the Republican Party – and the nation – for his own benefit.

In these pages, we've chronicled many of these developments and offered our perspective as these historic events unfolded. We will continue to do so.

We invite you to become a regular reader, subscriber or member of Lean to the Left and to listen and subscribe to our podcast and on YouTube and major audio podcast channels.

Just visit Lean to the Left.net and sign up. Don't worry, it's all free. For our podcasts, just click on the Podcast tab at the top of the home page. We offer interviews with experts and newsmakers, as well as people with interesting stories to tell. You can find us on YouTube at https://www.youtube.com/@LeantotheLeft.

We hope you enjoyed Hijacked Nation and will join us at Leantotheleft.net.

Acknowledgements

My thanks to our loyal Lean to the Left readers and listeners on our Lean to the Left podcast. Your encouragement and support keep us going as we seek to shed some light on the major developments that continue to shape our nation.

I also want to express my appreciation V. Susan Hutchinson for her important contributions that enrich our content.

The co-author of this book, C J (Chris) Waldron, is incredible. His insight into the issues and his determination to use his talents to help affect needed changes are evident in his essays. Chris pulls no punches and refuses to quit. Our job, he says, "is to preserve American ideals until America comes to its senses." Thank you, Chris, for your friendship and your dedication to this enterprise.

Finally, to my wife, Jackie, my thanks for putting up with my Lean to the Left obsession. Without her support, this project would never have happened. -- *Bob Gatty*

Books by Bob Gatty

Hijacked Nation, volumes one and two were published in 2020 and track the Trump presidency since 2018, organized by issue topic.

They are dedicated to all those who are fighting to save our nation from Donald Trump and his MAGA Republican sycophants who have hijacked the Republican Party and are attempting to do so to our nation.

This book is a sequel to those volumes. All can be found at Amazon. com.

◆◆◆

Baking Bread for the GENIUS-Secrets from a pro for your home kitchen was co-authored with Chef Brandon Cristiano and is intended to invite and encourage those who always wanted to bake bread at home but hesitated to do so because they feared the process was too complicated.

The book also is written for those with some experience in the bread-baking process who are looking for new ideas, new recipes, and new techniques.

It is filled with wonderful, easy-to-make recipes blended with tales of Chef Brandon's adventures as he has traveled the world.

It is available at Amazon.com.

About the Authors

Bob Gatty

Bob Gatty is the founder of the blog site Not Fake News, established in 2017 in response to Donald Trump's constant complaining about "fake news" and calling members of the media "the enemy of the people."

That site was renamed Lean to the Left and then in 2020 our Lean to the Left podcast was created, featuring political commentary and interviews that focus on progressive politics and the key social issues of our time.

Bob's career has included reporting for newspapers, managing a state capitol national wire service bureau, and covering Washington for several national business publications.

His company, G-Net Strategic Communications, assisted numerous national trade associations with their publications and communications needs. He is a journalist, editor, scriptwriter, speechwriter, photographer, and podcast host.

Bob now lives in Myrtle Beach, SC with his wife, Jackie.

CJ Waldron

Chris is from Schenectady, NY, and now lives in Conway, SC. He earned degrees in English and Political Science from the University of New York. For almost 30 years, he taught public school in Schenectady as an English and Special Education teacher. He has continued his career as an educator, currently as an adjunct instructor at Horry Georgetown Technical College.

218

Chris has served as a poll reporter and worked on political campaigns in New York state. He assisted the presidential campaigns of Bill Clinton, John Kerry, Hillary Clinton and Barack Obama with "Get Out the Vote" efforts.

An astute political analyst, Chris continues to be active in politics, supporting local, state and national Democratic candidates.

Chris writes with knowledge, insight and perspective as he analyzes important developments and shares his thoughts with Lean to the Left readers.

"Our job," he says, "is to preserve American ideals until America comes to its senses."

V. Susan Hutchinson

A guest contributor to this book, Susan is a native of Chicago. Susan earned a BS degree in Medical Technology from Northern Illinois University and held laboratory positions in Valdosta and Savannah, GA, Baltimore/DC and Dallas, TX before landing in the San Francisco area with a global company that sells clinical laboratory equipment and test kits.

She held training positions there and then worked in England as Regional Product Manager before returning to California in a management position in a global product support group. Susan took early retirement after 18 years with the company.

Susan moved to Conway, SC in January 2017 where she volunteers with AARP and is a member of the state AARP Executive Council. She volunteers with the Horry County, SC, Democratic Party, using her skills to support Party efforts.

Susan was a major contributor to initial two-volume *Hijacked Nation: Donald Trump's Attack on America's Greatness.*

Milton Keynes UK
Ingram Content Group UK Ltd.
UKHW050221021124
450572UK00004B/18